# ABILITY, INEQUALITY AND POST-PANDEMIC SCHOOLS

## Rethinking Contemporary Myths of Meritocracy

Alice Bradbury

P

First published in Great Britain in 2021 by

Policy Press, an imprint of
Bristol University Press
University of Bristol
1–9 Old Park Hill
Bristol
BS2 8BB
UK
t: +44 (0)117 954 5940
e: bup-info@bristol.ac.uk

Details of international sales and distribution partners are available at
policy.bristoluniversitypress.co.uk

British Library Cataloguing in Publication Data
A catalogue record for this book is available from the British Library

ISBN 978-1-4473-4661-6 hardcover
ISBN 978-1-4473-4702-6 paperback
ISBN 978-1-4473-4703-3 ePub
ISBN 978-1-4473-4701-9 ePdf

Cover design: Robin Hawes
Front cover image: iStock/alashi

For Amber, Jasmine and Lily

# Contents

# List of figures and tables

## Figures

## Tables

# Acknowledgements

First of all, I wish to thank my colleagues in the Centre for Sociology of Education and Equity, particularly Louise Archer, Stephen Ball, Annette Braun and Carol Vincent, for their support and advice during the writing of this book, and to my wider colleagues in the centre for taking on some extra work to allow me to take the sabbatical that made this book possible. I appreciate this collaborative community greatly.

I am grateful for the helpful conversations with Isobel Bainton and Laura Vickers-Rendall at Policy Press which guided where this book should go, and the support of the wider team at Policy Press in the publication process.

I wish to thank the National Education Union for funding the Grouping Project research discussed in this book. The unnamed participants of the research study discussed here – teachers, parents and school leaders – made a huge contribution to my thinking about 'ability'. My colleague Guy Roberts-Holmes, with whom I collaborated on the Grouping Project, and my wider network of people interested in 'ability' (particularly Eleanore Hargreaves, Emma Towers and Becky Taylor) also had an influence on the production of the arguments set out here. I am pleased to remain part of a culture at the UCL Institute of Education where challenging concepts such as 'ability' for the purposes of social justice is seen as important.

I am also grateful for the insights of my doctoral students on early versions of some chapters and for their general enthusiasm for the field, and to my past PhD student Valentina Migliarini for educating me about the complexities and usefulness of DisCrit. Some of the discussion here also builds on my work with my friends and colleagues Ian McGimpsey and Diego Santori on neuroscience. Some of the speculation about the impact of COVID-19 is informed by discussions with my colleagues at the UCL Institute of Education during this period, within the Helen Hamlyn Centre for Pedagogy, namely Yana Manyukhina and Dominic Wyse, and more widely, particularly my colleagues on the Economic and Social Research Council-funded *Duty of Care and Duty to Teach* project (ES/V00414X/1): Sam Duncan, Sinead Harmey, Rachel Levy and Gemma Moss. All errors are of course my own.

I wish also to thank the staff and volunteers of the Enfield Library Service, whose friendly and helpful service to my local community – and provision of a quiet place to write for those of us with noisy homes – is very much appreciated.

On a more personal note, I remain indebted to those around me who enable me to function as an academic with small children, particularly my mother and my parents-in-law, who were sorely missed during some of the writing of this book during the COVID-19 pandemic. The encouragement of friends, and particularly my fellow writer Helen Ochyra, has also been vital. This book has been met by many barriers, not least severe morning sickness, a new baby and a global pandemic; it has evolved with the changing times. It was begun as one daughter started school, bringing into sharp relief the themes from my own research, and completed as a second daughter begins Reception. My daughters keep me alive to the real consequences of the topics I research, and I hope that grounding helps me to write about what really matters for children far less privileged than my own. Finally, I am as ever thankful for the support of my husband Alistair, who always encourages me to take on new projects. The book is dedicated to our three children.

# 1

# Introduction

## Why 'ability' and inequality?

The main argument of this book is that the idea of 'ability' and how it operates is one of the ways in which the school system in England reproduces social inequalities, contrary to claims of meritocracy and fairness. This is not a new argument, but one that has been discussed in depth for decades, as academics have repeatedly made links between the idea of fixed intelligence and its damaging relation to particular social groups, including the working class and some minoritised communities (such as Gillborn 2010; Ball 2013). However, it is an argument that requires updating and contextualising in this post-pandemic era, where the disruption to normal ways of life has allowed for some disruption to 'normal' ways of thinking about schooling. What I aim to do here is to consider how these two axes of 'ability' and inequality operated in the era preceding the pandemic, in all their contextual peculiarity, and in turn to use this discussion to ask questions about the future, post-crisis education system.

This revisiting is necessary because discourse, as Foucault (1977) contends, operates in a particular historical and social context; thus we need to repeatedly consider how discourses of 'ability' and its proxies work to reproduce inequality in each period and context. I contend that the era under discussion – that of the late 2010s – requires particular scrutiny as the operation of 'ability' evolved in new directions. The political context of uncertainty related to Brexit, but where a 'Great Meritocracy' was imagined and equality of opportunity was idealised, provides a backdrop for this discussion of how current trends enliven the link between 'ability' and inequality; latterly, the uncertainties related to COVID-19 have produced fertile ground for debate over the role of schools in providing 'opportunity' throughout the population.

As Ladwig and McPherson have argued, teachers' concepts of ability 'have remained relatively unstudied' (2017, p. 344), despite their importance in contemporary education. Using data from a research project on grouping by 'ability', in this book I unpick contemporary discourses of ability and merit. This is my objective in writing this book: to illuminate how the idea of 'ability' has been reimagined, re-inscribed and reinvigorated by educational trends of the last decade. I focus on two particular themes which I argue have a fundamental impact on how we talk about and use 'ability' as a concept. These are, first, the influence of neuroscience and other biological ways of thinking about children's 'ability'; and second, the growth in the importance and use of data in schools, a phenomenon known as 'datafication' (Bradbury and Roberts-Holmes 2017c; Jarke and Breiter 2019b). In different ways, these two trends have altered how the discourse of 'ability' operates, and thus how it reproduces disadvantage. There is potential, I warn, in both of these two trends, for the discourse of *'ability' as fixed* to evolve in ways which further entrench inequality, and the post-pandemic era heightens this risk.

Before I turn in the rest of this introductory chapter to discussing the political context, the empirical work which I draw on here, and an outline of the book, I want to write about my own relationship to the term 'ability' (which hereafter, accepting that it is a contested and constructed term, I use without burdensome quote marks). Like many adults who were once children deemed 'successful' by the education system, I have an emotional investment in the idea of ability as something which some people possess a greater amount of. I was labelled a 'high ability' child from the moment I went to school, always on the reading scheme books ahead of everyone else and having to get my maths textbooks from the year above as I had exhausted the ones in my classroom. I have distinct memories of being on the Squares table in Year 1, which was, quite obviously to everyone, the 'top' table. I was never in a second set or group for my entire school career, through my community primary and comprehensive secondary school; never 'struggling' or 'behind'. I am undoubtedly the beneficiary of ability discourses, which only ever made me feel good about schoolwork (though they simultaneously marked me out as socially unacceptable as a teenager, but that is another story).

Looking back, however, I see this labelling as 'bright' in a different light. It was not until adulthood that I ever thought about how my school career might have been anything different from that of my peers. I was a white British child, born in September, and so I was tall and almost five years old when I started Reception. I had the benefit of living with a parent who taught me to read and write my name before I started school and an older sister already seen as 'bright', to whom I was constantly compared. Although I had a complicated family background and did not come from a wealthy home, my teachers must have recognised the essentially middle-class values of my book-loving single-parent father, who stayed at home full time and volunteered as a parent governor. In my socially and culturally mixed London primary, I now suspect how I was constructed in my Reception classroom: through discourses related to 'race', gender and class which positioned me as close to an ideal pupil. I have no doubt that this construction was a self-fulfilling prophesy, which in the contexts of the schools I attended, allowed me to be academically successful. Indeed, I see the pattern repeating in my two older daughters' starts to school life, as they benefit even more from the privileges of being white and decidedly middle class.

What I hope to illustrate through this discussion is how uncomfortable it can be to question the labels of 'bright' and 'high ability' when you are one of the 'winners' in the ability game. These are terms used so freely and liberally, even by those academics who research this field, that it can be a challenge to break beyond the constraints of this discourse and begin to question the very idea that some have more ability than others. This argument can also be misconstrued as an 'everyone is the same' simplification, so I should be clear here that I accept that some people are better at some things than others, and that this may be due to a mixture of both inherent and learnt characteristics. Instead, what I focus on is specifically *the idea of ability as fixed and generalisable intelligence, which we can recognise and measure*. I delve into the history of this idea in more detail in Chapters 2 and 3, but I begin here with the current political use of merit and ability.

## Merit and ability in recent political debate

### Government perspectives since 2010

> Whatever you may think of the value of IQ tests it is surely relevant to a conversation about equality that as many as 16% of our species have an IQ below 85. (Boris Johnson, cited in Watt 2013)

The Conservative and Conservative-led governments of the 2010s engaged with a vision of meritocracy that was simple and engaging: work hard and you will succeed. The 2010 manifesto talked of improving schools 'to make opportunity more equal and address our declining social mobility' (Conservative Party 2010). David Cameron's governments 2010–15 (in coalition with the Liberal Democrats) and 2015–16 had a focus on increasing opportunity for those most disadvantaged through measures such as the Pupil Premium, which provided additional funding for children in receipt of free school meals (FSM) in the last six years and children who are in local authority care or have been in the past (DfE 2013). The rhetoric of this period centred on 'restor[ing] rigour to the curriculum and exam system' (Conservative Party 2010) and opening more new schools to allow every child to succeed.

With even more emphasis on meritocracy, Theresa May, on becoming prime minister in July 2016, stood outside Downing Street and declared that her mission was 'to make Britain a country that works for everyone' (May 2016b). May's vision of a 'Great Meritocracy' was summed up in her Downing Street speech as 'We will do everything we can to help anybody, whatever your background, to go as far as your talents will take you'. In one of her first major speeches she explained:

> I want ‚Britain to be the world's great meritocracy – a country where everyone has a fair chance to go as far as their talent and their hard work will allow. I want us to be a country where everyone plays by the same rules; where ordinary, working class people have more control over their lives and the chance to share fairly in the prosperity of the nation. And I want Britain to be a place where advantage is based on merit not privilege; where it's your talent and hard work that matter, not where you were born, who your parents are or what your accent sounds like. Let us not underestimate what it will take to create that great meritocracy. It means taking on some big challenges, tackling some vested interests. Overcoming barriers that have been constructed over many years. It means not being afraid to think differently about what disadvantage means, who we want to help and how we can help them. Because where once we reached for simple ways of labelling people disadvantaged and were quick to pose simple – and often fairly blunt – solutions, in these modern times disadvantage is much more complex. It's often hidden and less easy to identify. It's caused by factors that are more indirect and tougher to tackle than ever before. But tackle it we must if we are to give ordinary, working class people the better deal they deserve. (May 2016a)

This vision, which includes both an attempt to broaden the notion of 'disadvantage' and a recourse to the phrase 'ordinary, working-class people', provides an attractive picture where imbalances are addressed without 'blunt' solutions and everyone benefits from a 'better deal'. Success is built on 'talent and hard work', not parental background or accent. Within this, there is re-inscription of the 'bright working-class student' discourse, so clear in the grammar school debates and the previous Conservative government. But by naming meritocracy as an ideal specifically and her repeated references to 'talents', May reinvigorated the idea that some are gifted, and the purpose of the education system is to allow this to flourish, independent of a child's background.

Ultimately May's domestic agenda was overshadowed as government struggled with the problem of Brexit, and she was replaced by Boris Johnson in the summer of 2019. The new prime minister, and the shift in the influence of the right within the Conservative Party, did not appear to alter the reliance on the discourse of meritocracy. The Conservative manifesto for the general election of December 2019 included 'Boris Johnson's guarantee' that he would 'unleash the potential of our whole country' (Conservative Party 2019). The introductory summary stated 'We will build a Britain in which everyone has the opportunity to make the most of their talents', continuing May's choice of the language of opportunity and talent. It went on:

> Talent and genius are uniformly distributed throughout the country. Opportunity is not. Now is the time to close that gap – not just because it makes such obvious economic sense, but for the sake of simple social justice.
>
> We Conservatives believe passionately that every child should have the same opportunity to express their talents and make the most of their lives – and that is why we are investing £14 billion over three years to increase funding for every primary and every secondary school pupil in the country. (Conservative Party 2019, p. 2)

Boris Johnson himself infamously stated, somewhat bluntly, that 'as many as 16% of our species have an IQ below 85' back in 2013, suggesting a belief in measurable and fixed intelligence. He also said 'The harder you shake the pack, the easier it will be for some cornflakes to get to the top', suggesting a purpose for education in 'sorting' those with more talent, because people are 'very far from equal in raw ability' (cited in Millar 2020). However, the discourse of *opportunity* remained the primary message in the Conservative campaign under his leadership. In this vision, providing opportunity through increasing funding allows the 'talent' to shine through. In terms of policy, the manifesto included plans to build more free schools and other 'innovative' schools, without mentioning the May era's most notable education policy, on grammar school expansion.

On coming to power, Johnson's government was focused initially on signing the Brexit withdrawal agreement, and after the late 2019 election delivered a majority and resolved the Brexit deadlock, the new government's agenda was entirely overtaken by the COVID-19 crisis. During the first lockdown period of spring 2020, the issue of inequity as a result of different experiences at home remained politically important, however. The discussion of reopening schools in the autumn frequently made reference to the problem of increasing the 'gap' between the attainment of rich and poor, and indeed the problem of 'learning loss' for disadvantaged pupils was given as a justification for the reopening of schools in June 2020. The Secretary of State for Education, Gavin Williamson, argued:

> The poorest children, the most disadvantaged children, the children who do not always have support they need at home, will be the ones who will fall furthest behind if we keep school gates closed. They are the ones who will miss out on the opportunities and chances in life that we want all children to benefit from what teachers and schools deliver for them. (Williamson 2020)

In this understanding of the education system, schools are there to deliver opportunity, to make up for the differences in 'support at home'. There is some recognition of structural difference, but simultaneously education is there to provide 'chances in life', with a subtext that chances must of course be taken, for example by sending your child to school.

### The opposition view: the rejection of caution

Opposition to ideas of fixed measurable intelligence have often been associated with the left (as I discuss further in the following chapters), but in recent decades many Labour politicians have come to accept a degree of meritocratic discourse or actively engage with a similar discourses of 'letting talent rise to the top', as seen earlier. This acceptance of meritocracy was apparent in the New Labour years: in a speech launching the Labour education manifesto for the 2001 election, Tony Blair talked of their aim that 'the secondary school of the future develops the talent of each individual pupil as far as it will go' (Blair 2001). He went on:

we want much more differentiated provision within schools
to meet the aptitudes and abilities of individual pupils.
More challenge for the very able, including accelerated
entry for GCSEs and other programmes to support them.
More support for the basics, targeted at pupils who arrive
at secondary school at risk of falling behind. (Blair 2001)

This idea that the system must cater for the various 'aptitudes and
abilities', from the very able to those 'at risk of falling behind', can be
seen as the predecessor to the meritocracy discourse of the Conservative
governments of the 2010s, and beyond (Littler 2017).

Even when the Labour Party shifted to the left under Jeremy Corbyn
after 2015, there were continued signs of an acceptance of meritocracy.
Notably, Tristam Hunt, during his time as Shadow Secretary of State
for Education, attempted to position the Labour Party as supportive of
children labelled 'gifted and talented'. In a 2015 article in the Guardian,
Hunt commented: 'There is nothing wrong in recognising that people
are born with different talents. We need to develop all talents, but it
is right to recognise that some talents can be stretched further' (cited
in Wintour 2015). Explaining his suggestion of an additional fund to
provide advice for teachers on how to 'stretch the most talented', Hunt
positions those who question the idea of ability as too cautious, or too
'politically correct' perhaps. The political editor who wrote the piece
described this argument as Hunt saying Labour must 'challenge its own
taboos', suggesting the idea of the 'highly able' is unacceptable on the
left. Hunt's comments are reinforced by quotes from Sir Peter Lampl
from the Sutton Trust, who refers to the state of 'provision for the
highly able' and similarly makes a link between supporting the most
able and the meritocratic ideal of 'bright young people from low- and
middle-income families'. In this discourse, supporting the 'most able' is
a social justice issue, mistakenly regarded as problematic by those with
what Hunt calls 'misplaced scruples'; indeed, a lack of support is 'an
underappreciated component of inequity' (Wintour 2015).

This attempt to reposition Labour as supportive of the 'highly able'
and thus the idea that ability is fixed and measurable through a social
justice discourse of helping the 'bright poor kids' shows the complexity
of political debate on this issue. Hunt was clearly keen to challenge
some long-established concerns about ability on the left, and perhaps
attempt to displace the Conservatives as the party most protective of
the 'highly able' child. The problematisation of ability is positioned as
well meaning but misguided and potentially damaging to the 'bright
young people' from poorer backgrounds. Dissent from the idea of

ability is dismissed, while the links between ability discourses and the perpetuation of inequality are obfuscated.

Of course, Labour moved further to the left in the later 2010s; more centrist ministers such as Tristam Hunt were replaced by more Corbynite loyalists, and the tone of Labour policy shifted. But, in the 2019 manifesto there were references to an education system which 'lets people develop their talents', and a promise of an education system which 'will nurture every child and adult to find a path that's right for them, by promoting all types of learning, skill and knowledge – technical, vocational, academic and creative' (Labour Party 2019). Corbyn's successor, Sir Keir Starmer, who was elected during the COVID-19 crisis, used similar language in his pledge to 'Pull down obstacles that limit opportunities and talent' in his campaign (Starmer 2020).

In conclusion, we see how from both sides of the political equation, the idea of a meritocratic education system which recognises talent and ability, combined with effort, and rewards this with success, has in the recent past dominated discussion of education's purpose and aims. The idea that meritocracy or ability themselves could be tools for the reproduction of inequality is largely absent. These political debates are the backdrop to the discourses of ability used in schools, which are my focus here, providing legitimacy and making the idea of meritocracy 'common-sense'.

## Theoretical perspectives

In this section I briefly set out some of the theoretical perspectives I draw on in this book. I am cautious here to avoid, as a colleague suggested, 'going all Foucault' on the reader. Undeniably, I could write an entire book on the disciplinary and regulatory functions of intelligence as an idea, using Foucault as a theoretical frame, but these discussions have been rehearsed elsewhere by those far more qualified and Foucauldian than me (Ball 2013). There are some key points I wish to outline here, however, from Foucault and from Critical Race Theory, which I think are helpful in making sense of the discussions in later chapters.

### Discourse and power

Throughout this book I argue that ability is a contemporary discourse of power which serves to reinforce social and racial inequalities in education. This argument is grounded in poststructural theory, particularly the work of Foucault, which focuses on the production of particular truths, such as the scientific concept of fixed and inheritable intelligence, and their maintenance. Discourses are productive, creating the very things they speak of, and establishing what constitutes truth. Thus discourses are a methods of reproducing rules and regularities: Foucault encourages us to think about 'how a particular discourse acquires status of scientificity, how it creates, in itself, so to speak, the conditions of what counts as truth' (Ball 2013, p. 5).

To put this argument more simply, I argue here that ability as discourse is a set of parameters which define and maintain acceptable truths. For example:

- that some are bright, some not;
- that nature vs nurture is the main problematic of intelligence;
- that we have talents;
- that we all 'develop' (though not in linear fashions) and there are variations in the speed and extent of this development which we can recognise;
- that we can measure or assess ability, and so compare child against child.

In thinking about discourse in this way, we also need to consider the different relationship groups of people have to the production of knowledge and truth; that is, that some have the power to define truths, while others do not. As Ball writes, 'Knowledges are produced within power relations also in the sense that some groups or institutions have been able to speak *knowledgeably about* "others", subaltern groups, who were concomitantly rendered silent' (Ball 2013, p. 15). These truths have not been defined by children, or even teachers or parents, but by particular groups of power holders, who, over a long period, established these ideas so that they appear self-evident. The analysis of how this happens is described by Foucault as genealogy: 'The task is to find out how a human being was envisaged in a particular period and the social practices that constituted this human being' (Ball 2013, p. 35). This task is not about finding determinations or limits, but the 'unmaking of solidity and inevitability, creating the possibilities for transgression' (Ball 2013, p. 35). Thus genealogy allows for thinking otherwise about key concepts such as human intelligence.

Perhaps then, this book could be described as a genealogy of the rules and regulations that drive ability at the present time. The remaining chapters ask: what does this discourse do while it is there? What does it make possible, and what continues to make it possible and feasible?

## Discipline and regulation

Using Foucault's idea of two techniques of power, disciplinary and regulatory, Ball (2013) adumbrates two histories of education policy: a history of classifications, and a history of blood, related to Foucault's two politics. These historical perspectives are outlined in Chapter 2, but here it is important to distinguish between discipline (anatamo-politics), which works on the individual, and regulation (biopolitics), which works on the population. 'The regulatory (biopower) and the disciplinary operate at different levels, what we might roughly call policy and practice, but which are closely interrelated at many points' (Ball 2013, p. 60).

The concept of disciplinary power focuses on the individual, on the 'micro' rather than on the 'macro' of structures. This is power that is invisible and pervasive, 'circulating rather than being possessed, productive and not necessarily repressive' (Gore 1995, p. 167). It works on the individual be making them visible and knowable; discipline 'analyses and breaks down; it breaks down individuals, places, time, movements, actions and operations. It breaks them down into components such that they can be seen, on the one hand, and modified on the other' (Foucault, 2009, p. 56, cited in Ball 2013, p. 46).

Regulatory power, in contrast, considers the social body as a whole. Biopolitics 'refers to a positive and encouraging mode of government':

> In biopolitics, life – the biological capacities and skills of individuals in particular, and the conducts and properties of population in general – appears as an object of political strategies that are not negative in nature (such as punishing, disciplining, prohibiting, or about the menace of death). Instead, political strategies operate as a positive force that forms, shapes, fosters, develops and administers life in order to gain maximum benefit out of it. (Millei and Joronen 2016, p. 391)

I have not always been as precise as necessary in using these two forms of power and politics, but here I want to use the division productively to consider further the power of the norm. As Ball argues, 'the school is one of those places where the body and population meet' and the norm works across both, linking these two poles of disciplinary and regulatory power through relations including 'the teacher, the test, grouping by ability, special schooling, "race" and class' (Ball 2013, p. 54). Normalisation – the comparison of all against a set standard – represents a key micropractice of power within the classroom (Gore 1995), which is combined with classification and distribution – the labelling of children and their allocation to groups or sets. In sum, these practices are disciplinary, confining children to paths of educational success or failure. But the norm also operates on a broader basis in relation to the population, which is also subject to the application of the norm.

> The norm, and its intertwined moral and statistical applications, provided a scientific basis for the measurement and judgement 'double', a 'grid of intelligibility' within which individuals could be categorized and compared in relation to one another, and in relation to the national interest, and the management of the population as a resource. (Ball 2013, p. 61)

This need to manage the population for productivity means in education allocating resources in efficient ways. This requires some differentiation between those deemed 'educable' from the 'non-educable', based on norms informed by scientific conceptions of 'intelligence', as discussed further in Chapter 2. As Hunter comments, the population is seen as 'the bearer of an array of conducts and capacities that had been rendered problematic through application of statistically determined norms and standards of living' (Hunter 1996, p. 154, cited in Ball 2013, p. 59).

Thus we see the norms associated with ability traditionally working in *both* disciplinary and regulatory ways – in the classroom through grouping practices and within the population through policies which label and allocate some to alternative educational provision, or exclude them altogether as 'impossible bodies' (Youdell 2006). We see the management of the population in terms of progression through education, in discussions of the allocation of qualifications to certain proportions of the population and the proportion of people who should go on to university. We saw regulatory discourse in discussion of how children from poorer backgrounds needed to return to school after the pandemic, as the gap between rich and poor children's attainment was described as increasing due to school closures (EEF 2020). This was based on the norms of expected progress and attainment: here children are 'living resources, where the aim of government is to control the health, welfare and conducts of children in such as a manner that the overall productivity of life can be increased' (Millei and Joronen 2016, p. 391). This level of analysis can easily be forgotten in discussion of how schools operate, but throughout this book the discussion aims to consider both disciplinary and regulatory functions of the discourse of ability, and particularly their entwinement with the norm.

### Micropractices of power: classification and normalisation

A further Foucault-influenced theoretical tool based on disciplinary power I use here is the idea of micropractices, developed in Jennifer Gore's (2001) work on classroom practices. Gore draws on Foucauldian concepts to provide a schema of ways in which power operates through often apparently neutral practices. For her, disciplinary power takes the form of micropractices of power which constitute the 'pedagogical regime'. The discussion of micropractices, I would argue, aids recognition of the complexities of power as it operates in classrooms, and draws our attention to the importance of activities which appear 'normal'. In particular, Gore's description of *classification*, the use of truths to distinguish between children, is important here, as I consider how the idea that ability is measurable facilitates the allocation of children to groups. As Ball has argued, these classifications imply fundamental differences between children, although they appear to simply be determined by practicality or convenience: 'Schools systems, with few exceptions are rooted in a history of classifications and differentiations, in particular those that are articulated by performance, which is taken to be an indicator of something deeper – ability' (Ball 2013, p. 51).

Also relevant are the micropractices of *distribution*, the use of truths to organise people physically in a space, such as in groups or sets based on the idea of measurable and fixed ability; and also *exclusion*, which is the use of truths to create boundaries of normality and abnormality. These two micropractices are useful in thinking about the two trends I focus on here. As I discuss in Chapter 5, datafication works in tandem with *distribution*, as data are used to organise children on spreadsheets and in classrooms. Meanwhile ideas from neuroscience justify processes of *exclusion* (and also the connected micropractice of *normalisation*) and some children are deemed incapable of learning. Thus Gore's terms, I contend, provide useful a shorthand for the examination of the everyday, seemingly benign and common-sense practices of a school as shaped by power and particular 'truths'.

### Inequality and inequity

The other major area of concern in this book – inequality – is theoretically underpinned by various perspectives on the reproduction of inequalities in education and society more generally. I use Critical Race Theory (CRT), the body of work on racial inequity originating in the US, as an influencing position here, rather than as a primary theoretical source. While I use CRT extensively in other work, I would hesitate to describe this discussion as a CRT piece, as the focus is broader and I do not place 'race'[1] at the centre, in this case. Instead, what I take from CRT and its use in education (see Dixson and Rousseau 2006; Gillborn 2006a; Edward Taylor et al 2009) is a perspective where the focus is on the 'taken for granted' and 'normal' ways racism operates. CRT scholars examine the 'business as usual' (Bell 1992) forms of racism, which are not redressed through law; in education, these include, for example, the way in which the curriculum denies the importance of some communities' cultures and histories or the prioritisation of funding for schools in white areas over those in communities of colour (Ladson-Billings 2004); and the influence on minoritised students of reform of methods of school accountability (Gillborn et al 2018). In many cases, policies which are not explicitly related to issues of inequality have the consequence of exacerbating differences between groups of students (Gillborn 2006b; Gillborn et al 2018). I have used this focus in my own work on teacher assessment in the early years to explore how low expectations of young children from minoritised and economically disadvantaged communities are reinforced by national data from assessments, producing a situation where anything but below average results are unintelligible for a 'difficult intake' of children in an inner city school (Bradbury 2013b). Starting from a position of interrogating the 'normal' in relation to inequality reveals the complexities but also the banality of many of the practices and policies which have significant impacts on children's lives.

This focus on the everyday workings of the education system as the site where inequalities are produced, reproduced and maintained differs from traditional forms of CRT in that I am equally interested in the operation of class (as, indeed, are other CRT-influenced discussions such as Rollock et al 2015). The reasoning for this is that, to put it simply, *both* class and race matter in the English education system. Other aspects of identity and differentiation matter too, of course – gender and dis/abilty most notably – but are not my main focus here. Various parts of this book concentrate more closely on race or class, with an awareness that these and other elements of identity intersect.

A further point of theoretical importance here is the influence of Disability Critical Race Studies, or DisCrit (Annamma et al 2013; Annamma et al 2018), which is an off-shoot of CRT that combines discussion of racism with ideas from disability studies. DisCrit alerts us to the relationships between racial inequity and the labelling of some children as 'disabled' or with special educational needs and disabilities (SEND), using a medical model of disability. A central premise is to challenge the fixity and permanence of the concept of disability (Annamma et al 2018). Although my focus here is not, in the main, on the classification of some children as having SEND, this is clearly a part of the general classificatory systems in operation in schools, and recognising the importance of dis/ability studies in how we understand processes of classification is important. DisCrit does not only focus on this area – the school-to-prison pipeline and the role of school reform are also important foci – but there is an overriding concern with the intersection of race, class and the dividing practices associated with concepts of dis/ability (Annamma et al 2018). Research from around the world has shown how children from certain groups are disproportionately labelled as SEND (Migliarini et al 2020); indeed, a text concerned with Caribbean children's over-representation in schools for the 'educationally sub-normal' is one of the first major texts in the sociology of race and education (Coard 1971). DisCrit scholars have pointed to the pernicious effects of this labelling on students of colour and the ways in which this reproduces structural disadvantages (Annamma 2016). More recent data from England suggests that this continues to be the case, as Black Caribbean boys are disproportionately labelled as having social, emotional and mental health needs, even when socio-economic status and prior attainment are accounted for (Strand and Lindorff 2018). This system of classification into a binary of SEND/normal works alongside and in a mutually reinforcing relationship with broader notions of the spectrum of fixed abilities, and DisCrit provides some tools for analysis of the complexity of these discourses in education. I return to this topic, and the broader theoretical terrain, in more detail in Chapter 3.

## Contemporary educational discourses: data and neuroscience

As explained, the logic of focusing on ability in the contemporary era is motivated by a concern about how the notion of ability is being used in ways which both reproduce and justify inequality. Like many others (Gillborn 2010, 2016; Dorling and Tomlinson 2016), I want to draw attention to the ways in which scientific and technological developments are reviving and reimagining the idea of fixed, inherited and measurable intelligence, while at the same time parallel developments are being used to reconfigure classed and raced disparities as produced through an interaction between genes and environment, including types of parenting. Following Meloni's (2017) argument, and others who have written on the translation of science into the social and policy world, I argue that there is no inevitable path which these adoptions will take; instead, how 'new knowledges' are used and mobilised is dependent on political and ethical decisions (McGimpsey et al 2017). It is by uncovering the choices that are made, through scrutiny of the impact of new developments, that we can bring into question the connections made between, for example, home lives and damaged brains, or the idea that we can measure the potential of young children. The post-pandemic world, where so much of what we thought was inevitable has been upended, makes this questioning more urgent and allows for a broader debate.

The two trends I examine here have emerged from the findings of my research in schools and on policy in the last few years. First, the importance of data is an area I have explored in relation to statutory assessment in early years with my colleague Guy Roberts-Holmes (Bradbury and Roberts-Holmes 2017c), and the field of data and education is an area under increasing scrutiny as technological developments alter practice and values (for example, Williamson 2015; Selwyn 2016b), particularly following the pandemic (Williamson et al 2020b). The data under discussion are mainly those related to attainment, but the field increasingly includes research on how data on children's behaviour, 'mindsets' and attitudes are recorded (Williamson 2017). The importance of data is also inextricably linked with neoliberal systems of accountability, which are evolving in the 'late neoliberal' era (McGimpscy 2016). The COVID-19 pandemic, with the focus on the use of technology in education during homeschooling, added a further dimension to this datafication, as for a period teaching and learning were mediated by technology, and thus produced new forms of data and analytics (Williamson et al 2020b) which are only beginning to be examined.

I began to explore the second trend – the influence of neuroscience – in work examining how 'new knowledges' translate into education policy, with Ian McGimpsey and Diego Santori (see McGimpsey et al 2017). Like many other academics interested in early years, I was alarmed at the use of ideas presented as neuroscience to justify policies of 'early intervention' (Edwards et al 2015; Gillies et al 2017). In a 2017 article, we explained the use (or abuse) of neuroscience as an example of how politicians could use 'new knowledges' to alter the subject of policy, emphasising individual responsibility for how some children 'develop'. I extend this discussion further here by making links between this use of neuroscience and the concept of ability, and by also introducing other 'biological' ways of understanding children (Youdell 2017) into this discussion. This trend toward the neuro/biologisation of the child was also altered by the COVID-19 crisis, as the discourse around children's experiences focused on their mental health, resilience and the impact on learning of the trauma some children experienced (see, for example, NEU 2020; The National College 2020).

The decision to focus on these trends is based, therefore, both on areas which have long been topics of concern in my and others' work, and on ideas emerging from empirical work, which have in turn been altered by the effects of the global pandemic on education. I now turn to an explanation of the research project that originally motivated this argument, which I hope provides a thread of 'real life' running through the book.

## Researching ability

The sections of this book which draw on empirical data were developed from a project I co-led with Guy Roberts-Holmes in 2017, titled 'Grouping in Early Years and Key Stage 1', funded by the National Education Union (NEU) (which is the UK's largest trade union for teachers) (Bradbury and Roberts-Holmes 2017b).

The project arose out of a concern from the NEU over the impact of recent policy developments in the early phases of primary schools on classroom practices. At the time, there was also growing concern over the impact of grouping by ability or 'attainment', arising from the much larger-scale project on grouping in secondary education, also based at the UCL Institute of Education (Francis et al 2019). This project was intended to explore what was happening in classrooms from ages three to seven, to add to the contemporary understanding of policy and practice. We began by conducting four focus groups with teachers who were NEU members, to explore key issues relating to grouping. This led to some refinement of the areas of concern (particularly, a focus on phonics was identified as important in these focus group discussions). We then conducted a nationwide online survey using Opinio software, which had 1,373 responses. Table 1.1 shows a breakdown of the respondents to this survey by job role. The survey included a range of questions on how grouping was conducted, which subjects children were grouped for, and how decisions were

**Table 1.1:** Respondents to the Grouping Project survey by role

| Role | Percentage of respondents |
| --- | --- |
| Nursery teacher | 9 |
| Reception teacher | 22 |
| Year 1 teacher | 20 |
| Year 2 teacher | 18 |
| Support teacher | 2 |
| EY or KS1 phase leader | 14 |
| Deputy or headteacher | 4 |
| Support staff | 4 |
| Other | 7 |

made. Teachers were also asked their views on grouping and on the term 'ability'. These written survey comments are denoted by the letter W.

Following the survey, we conducted interviews at four case study schools in different regions of the UK. This was an opportunistic sample, based on accessing different localities, types and sizes of school and different attitudes to grouping. We interviewed class teachers and/or school leaders in each school, depending on availability, and asked them about their practices and reasons for their choices.

The names of all participants and schools have been changed, and titles are deliberately vague to ensure anonymity. The research was conducted in line with the British Education Research Association guidelines and approved by the University College London ethical review board.

Data were collated using NVivo and Excel, and analysed with the help of our research assistant, Mary-Claire Travers. The findings were reported on at the time (Bradbury and Roberts-Holmes 2017b), and we have subsequently written papers which draw on this work (Bradbury 2018b; Roberts-Holmes 2019). Here I make use of some of the data we collected to illuminate my arguments in relation to ability and inequality, though it should be noted that this was not the sole original focus of the project. This is not intended as a research monograph which recounts the findings of this project; rather, the data are used as ways in to thinking about how ability operates in the contemporary education system. I also make occasional reference to other research projects, such as my work on the impact of statutory tests; methods for these projects are explained in related publications.

## An outline of the book

The next two chapters set out the overall argument through an examination of key concepts, such as ability, and how this relates to inequality; these are followed by a chapters on the influence of neuroscience and datafication, and a concluding chapter.

Chapter 2 asks two questions 'Why examine ability?', and 'How is 'ability' used in schools?'. It provides a more detailed explanation of the logic of focusing on one key concept and considering its operation at a particular historical time. This then leads on to an overview of the historical context for concepts of 'merit' and 'ability' and their relation to classed and raced expectations of educational success. The chapter also discusses what is particular about the current use of ability, drawing on research data drawn from a survey of over 1,000 teachers, where they were asked the meaning of the term 'ability'. Their responses are categorised in an attempt to unpick the complexity and 'slipperiness' of the term. It is argued that the very ambiguity of the term adds to its power as an organising concept which disadvantages some groups of students. Two key conceptions of ability emerge – ability as innate, and ability as positional. These two understandings are linked to the developments discussed in later chapters. Finally, the last section of Chapter 2 focuses on research data on how the terms are used in schools as justification for pedagogical practices such as ability grouping. Here I set out the findings from my own research on primary education and others' findings on secondary education to emphasise the importance of ability in the organisation of students in classrooms. It is argued that ability works powerfully to justify systems of grouping and labelling pupils, which limit expectation and attainment, often in inequitable ways.

Chapter 3 focuses on inequalities and how the idea of 'ability' relates to their maintenance and reproduction. It begins with an outline of current educational inequalities in England, from early years to secondary education, and the most prominent debates in the field of race and class in education. Then, data from the Grouping Project and other research projects are used to examine how ability interacts with inequalities, at all levels of the schooling system. Then I consider the resurgence of ideas which link intelligence levels with different social groups, known as the 'new eugenics', and the challenges posed by epigenetics to deterministic accounts of merit. I then consider how debates about inequalities in education have shifted and continue to change during the pandemic era.

Chapter 4 focuses on the first of the two developments under consideration, the influence of neuroscience. Using ideas from critical neuroscience, it explores how scientific developments in the 'new neuros' (Pykett 2012) have been presented as dramatic revolutionary alternations in how we understand human nature and potential, and how in turn these 'insights' have been translated into education. The turn to neuroscience in education has produced particular discourses about children, including an emphasis on the first three years as a vital period of development. The chapter considers the doubts and dangers of neuroscience and the critique from researchers in early childhood education especially, before considering the attractiveness of the field, and the power of the image of the brain scan. These developments are related to discourses of ability and inequalities in education through discussion of how a focus on the brain facilitates a conception of ability as biological, and how discourses of damaged brains present in policy re-inscribe conceptions of the brain as determined by background. I conclude that neuroscience as culturally constructed serves as a biopolitical frame for understanding different children's abilities and usefulness.

The second educational development of datafication is discussed in Chapter 5. Datafication is defined as an increase in the prominence and importance of data in schools, with an impact on practice, values and subjectivities. The different elements are described here as the five Ps of datafication: relating to pedagogy, practices, priorities, people and power. One result of datafication is that much of what teachers do is geared towards producing the right data, particularly in relation to demonstrating progress. The chapter explains how this has been fed by policy which reifics progress measures and an inspection regime which relies on data analysis. The chapter goes on to explore data-based ability practices, that is, the use of data to label and classify children into different levels or stages, which are then taken to be indicative of levels of 'ability'. Research data are used here as illustrations of these processes, with a particular focus on the significance of progress measures as systems which reduce children to data. It is argued that data have a disciplinary function and that data and ability as discursive formations are co-reliant: data shows ability, and different abilities produce the data. They are also both based on the principle of objective measurement as the best means to understand the child as learner.

The final chapter brings together this discussion of the two educational developments by considering their commonalities and points of difference, and how they coalesce in ways which allow for discourses of ability as fixed and measurable to be reinvigorated. The multiple conceptions of ability are discussed, and it is argued that the slippages between them do not preclude their combined impact of maintaining inequalities. I consider the 'winners' in the game of meritocracy, which is based on these discourses of ability, and the barriers to thinking differently about individuals. The chapter concludes by considering the future of ability and my post-pandemic hope that the crisis will alter priorities and practices, despite the continuation of the neoliberal ideology that underpins education policy, and the hope that the idea of ability as fixed and measurable – and the inequalities that result – can be disrupted.

# 2

# Ability and its use in schools

## Introduction

This chapter focuses on the concept of ability as it is currently used in schools. The main focus is on what we can glean from teachers' responses to a question about their understanding of 'ability' in the context of grouping decisions (arising from the Grouping Project explained in Chapter 1). As Ladwig and McPherson argue, there is research on the role of ability in distribution of curricula but 'teachers' conceptualisation and everyday use of the term "ability" has remained relatively obscure' (2017, p. 344). My intention here is to complement the existing literature on the concept of ability in policy and its dangerous effects by exploring the operation of this discourse at classroom (or disciplinary) level, through analysis of the words of teachers on the topic. A final section following the discussion of teachers' conceptions of ability considers the manifestation of ability in classroom practices, including grouping, labelling and interventions. These are the real-world effects of the ideas held by teachers.

Before embarking on this discussion, it is important to provide some historical context for the concept of ability and its related ideas of intelligence, potential and meritocracy. In the following sections, I examine how scholars have characterised the development of intelligence as an idea, and how it manifests itself in modern political and social discourses shaped by neoliberalism. I also consider how recent findings in genetics and epigenetics have influenced discussions about the hereditability of intelligence, in what has been called the 'postgenomic' era. I am guided in the following short endeavour into the history of ability by a concern not to oversimplify the evolution of the term nor create a neat linear trajectory; after all, ideas about intelligence have been contested at every stage. This pursuit – a mini-genealogy perhaps – is about recognising the broader context of the real focus of my discussion here, which is the present-day use of ability. As Ball explains, 'the task is to find out how a human being was envisaged in a particular period and the social practices that constituted this human being' (2013, p. 35). Others have presented far more detailed histories of these concepts, as referred to later, but it would be remiss not to reflect on the historical foundation of ability as a concept.

## The historical context

The term 'ability' as used in schools owes a great deal to the idea of intelligence; it is associated with being 'bright', 'clever' or the opposite. Intelligence is an idea much discussed in both the scientific and social scientific worlds, with far more complexity than can be achieved here. The modern understanding of intelligence is regarded as developing from Francis Galton's 1876 book *Hereditary Genius*, though there are clearly longer historical examples of this concept – White (2006) argues the idea arises from the sixteenth-century Protestant Reformation for example. Galton's book attempted to explain why some individuals were more successful than others and traced family connections between the 'highly able'. As a result, Galton (who was Darwin's second cousin, notably) defined intelligence as 'whatever it is that the upper class has more of' (Richardson 2017, p. 7). This led to tests of 'intelligence', which in turn developed into the IQ test, as Galton's ideas spread around the world and were taken up by Karl Pearson in the UK and Lewis Terman in the US. The sinister side of this work was present from the beginning: Galton founded the Eugenics Society, which sought to restrict reproduction for those with 'less potential', and later his ideas were the basis of anti-immigration policy in the US in the 1920s and the horrors of the Third Reich. While eugenic ideas were rejected in the post-war period due to this association with genocide, the idea of measurable intelligence continued to be acceptable (and has arguably enjoyed a resurgence as science has provided new evidence of innate differences [Richardson 2017], as discussed later).

The idea of innate measurable intelligence was mobilised in the organisation of education in England from the beginnings of the formal school system. In the late nineteenth century, 'a machinery of differentiation and classification' operated (Ball 2013, p. 44); systems of ranking pupils were commonplace, based on testing and examinations. The skill of classifying pupils, or recognising their place on a spectrum of ability, became part of a teacher's competence (Ball 2013). In the twentieth century, the idea of 'channelling abilities' grew in prominence (Ball 2013), based on the idea that every child possesses something different, which is best put to use in different ways. Based on the scientifically produced accuracy of IQ tests, and the 'naturalness' of ability, the idea that children could be measured as more or less intelligent resulted in a schooling system which divided children at 11 into grammar, secondary modern and technical schools (McCulloch 2016). Cyril Burt developed a system based on testing, which he saw as providing the right paths for all: 'Classifying children so that they followed the eugenically appropriate course for them was his lifetime's work' (White 2006, p. 21). In these developments, particularly Burt's 'simple' view of intelligence as an unquestionable idea, Chitty argues we can see the long-lasting influence of Galton (2011). Burt embraced 'the notion of innately determined limits, differing markedly from one individual to another and parallel to those in human bodily development' (Chitty 2011, p. 238); for him, intelligence was intellectual and general (not affective or specific).

The tripartite system, with its underpinnings in eugenic ideas (Lowe 1997) was for the most part dismantled in the late 1960s and 1970s. The questioning of the concept of fixed intelligence was central to the campaign for comprehensive schooling, according to Brian Simon. Literature such as Alice Heim's 1954 book *The Appraisal of Intelligence* and Simon's work criticised 'the unreal abstraction of cognitive ability form the whole human being in his or her environment' (Chitty 2011, p. 239). But we should not overstate the dismissal of the idea of fixed intelligence, Chitty argues, as there were 'still groups of diehard psychometrists and eugenicists in the 1960s and 1970s who remained committed to the concept of innate mental ability' (Chitty 2011, p. 242); for example, Arthur Jensen's 1969 paper 'How Much Can We Boost IQ and Scholastic Achievement?' related innate intelligence to class and race, with the conclusion that attempting to compensate for natural differences through government spending was pointless. This era when the 'the psychometrists fight back' demonstrates the persistence of these ideas, even in the progressive, comprehensive period of England's school system. Furthermore, key vestiges of the same principles remain today in areas where selective schools still exist, and of course in government policy on the expansion of grammar schools. We also see the influence of enduring ideas about ability as fixed in within-school policies such as streaming and setting (Bradbury 2018b; Francis et al 2019) and in interactions between teacher and pupil (Marks 2016). As I discuss in the following chapter, the history of 'ability' is a history of division and inequality: the idea of varying intelligence cannot be separated from its historical and contemporary relation to discourses of class and race.

So, what, then, is the idea of intelligence that emerged – or crystallised to use Meloni's (2017) phrase – from the twentieth century? A common theme in much writing about intelligence is the sheer impossibility of definition (Fletcher 2011; Richardson 2017).

Charles Spearman 'discovered' *g*, or *general intelligence*, in 1915 but admitted the idea was not well defined; Cyril Burt saw intelligence as 'innate, general, cognitive ability' when designing the eleven-plus (Burt 1955, p. 265, cited in White 2006, p. 11). The term continues to lack rigid definition, sometimes being conflated with potential, multiple intelligences or specific skills such as mathematical ability. But perhaps this ambiguity is central to the perpetuation of the idea; it is used in different ways in different contexts, and for different ages of individuals (Fletcher 2011). The lack of definition is also obscured by the apparent fixity of IQ tests, which provide data and comparisons and give the illusion that what they measure must exist. Many critics, of course, argue that what they measure is how good someone is at that test, as shown by the variations in results and the 'Flynn effect', which is the improvement in test results over time (Stobart 2008). As such, IQ is 'the deceptive tool of an inexact science looking for rather exact consequences' (Richardson 2017, p. 9). Intelligence testing is an example of how 'an assessment can create whatever it claims to measure' (Stobart 2008, p. 30):

> The history of intelligence testing reinforces the argument that assessment is a social activity, even though its advocates presented it as impartial scientific measurement. The leading figures were largely driven by their ideological beliefs, which themselves were based on hereditarian, racial and class assumptions. This historical baggage has found a place in our attitudes and vocabulary today. (Stobart 2008, p. 31)

Through the twentieth century, the idea of intelligence as something measurable and innate became 'common-sense', but depended on historical contingencies, rather than being an inevitable process (White 2006). Thus we must be conscious of the 'Galtonian thought-world that had come down to us via intelligence testing' (White 2006, p. 14), and how this shapes perceptions of human potential and educational trajectories. However attractive this neat narrative might be, the contestation over the idea of inherited intelligence must be acknowledged: there have been competing visions of heredity since the nineteenth century, related to different political positions, as described by Meloni (2017) in his 'roadmap to the epigenetic present'. 'Hard' versions of genetic determinism competed with views of 'soft' heredity where the other influences, such as education, are recognised (Youdell 2016, p. 792). There is no inevitability, Meloni argues, in the dominance of harder conceptions of heredity as evidenced by the eugenics movement; the importance placed on different scientific developments might have differed, had the moment 'crystallised' differently.

As Richardson argues, the ambiguity of concepts such as potential make them 'so prone to ideological infill and political rhetoric'; he argues that potential is 'an ideological convenience that perfectly maintains the notion of innate differences and limits while framing the contemporary rhetoric about "equal opportunities" and "fulfilling our children's potential"' (Richardson 2017, p. 6). Within a neoliberal meritocracy, as I discuss later, the result is a hopeful message that we might improve our lot, but there are also limits set by our genes: potential as an ideological construct 'subtly weaves hope and fatalism into our unequal societies' (Richardson 2017, p. 6).

## The meritocratic neoliberal state

The current operation of the concept of ability or intelligence can only be understood in political terms as part of the neoliberal state; '"ability" is central to notions of a meritocratic society' (Ladwig and McPherson 2017, p. 344). The influence since the 1970s of neoliberal ideas of the state and the individual shapes how the individual is seen as responsible for themselves and their family, while the state's role is minimal. The basic idea is that society functions as a meritocracy, where ability + effort = merit, and those with more merit rise to positions of power and wealth. The idea was originally presented by Michael Young as a satire in 1958 under very different circumstances from those of today (Allen 2011a), but has since been taken on board across the political spectrum. Littler (2017) traced the development of meritocracy in her book *Against Meritocracy*, arguing the current neoliberal version is now the only way in which the term is understood. This contrasts with a social-democratic version of meritocracy with a greater role for the state in helping those who suffer within a competitive system, a notion of meritocracy based on the welfare state and significant upward social mobility (Littler 2017). Instead, as Reay argues, in the contemporary era 'Meritocracy has become a key weapon in neoliberalism's armoury, the dominant ideology justifying neoliberalism's central tenet of "the winner takes all"' (2020b, p. 405).

Littler examines the development of this 'meritocratic feeling' through the neoliberal era. Under Thatcher, meritocracy was shaped by 'aspirational femininity in particular and a very bounded, individualised (and/or nuclear family-based) form of consumerism' (Littler 2017, p. 82). This is evidenced in the 'right to buy' policy, which allowed residents to buy their council houses, the era of 'conspicuous consumption' (such as that displayed by 'yuppies') and the association between consumption and empowerment, especially for working-class women. Under John Major in the 1990s – himself an example of success from a non-elite background – the nostalgic 'back to basics' agenda meant 'the "merit" of meritocracy was being profoundly gendered and racialised and was dependent on patriarchal family life for its "success"' (2017, p. 85). In this era, Littler argues, society was 'understood as being egalitarian enough' (2017, p. 85). Tony Blair, who used the term meritocracy more than other prime ministers, presided over a period where neoliberal marketisation was combined with social liberalism and welfare investment. Influenced by sociologist Anthony Giddens, New Labour policy sought to end the privileges of the elite and attempted to address inequalities through policies such as the minimum wage and extending paid parental leave. In education, a programme of Gifted and Talented provision aimed to provide for the 'most able'; this White (2006) sees as the latest iteration of Galton and Burt's project of identifying an intellectual elite and developing special provision for them. The persistence of fixed intelligence during this period is also seen in the former Chief Inspector of Schools Chris Woodhead's book *The Desolation of Learning* (2009), where he argued 'children are not equally intelligent, and some are not very intelligent at all' (p. 41, quoted in Chitty 2011, p. 243).

Blair's socially liberal form of meritocracy continued under Gordon Brown as prime minister and in some ways into the era of the Conservative–Liberal Democrat Coalition. However in this latter era, the politics of austerity meant that the 'language of meritocracy was deployed without the introduction of ameliorating initiatives or forms of collective provision' (Littler 2017, p. 89). Under Cameron, in the 'Aspiration Nation', the importance of hard work and individual dedication became only more prominent; after all, 'hope and promise become more integral in an unequal society in which hard work alone had less and less chance of reaping the prizes' (Littler 2017, p. 89). Throughout these different manifestations of meritocracy, Littler argues, the idea was regarded as 'unproblematically positive' (2017, p. 88), but this is an example of 'cruel optimism' (after Lauren Berlant), where it appears anyone can improve their situation just due to effort, but there are actually active impediments to progress. Her account takes us up to society under Theresa May, whose vision of the 'Great Meritocracy' was discussed in Chapter 1.

Littler's history of 'meritocratic feeling' reveals how the particularities of the term – and I would argue its component parts ability and effort – are shaped by the contingencies of the time. Particular leaders, ways of thinking evident in education policy and economic imperatives shape how the idea of meritocracy is formulated. While we may not engage in IQ tests, the ideas inherent within them still exist in the form of aptitude testing and the concept of ability (Stobart 2008). Ability, as an idea, is part of this meritocratic assemblage; it is a building block of the idea that we all succeed differently depending on our talents and effort. This is why in subsequent chapters I consider how current trends are influencing how we see ability; these are the current contingencies at play, alongside the political factors discussed earlier. My aim is to consider ability within the current *episteme*, to use Foucault's formulation; this is a structure of truth which 'establishes the conditions for any statement to be "within the true"' (Ball 2013, p. 21). I also consider how different 'truths' about ability produced by these trends relate to social and racial inequalities. In the late 2010s, for example, much of the blame for social disadvantage, and the related educational attainment gaps, was placed on parents and their provision of enabling 'home learning environments' (Hinds 2018); this 'truth' – that children's environments produce different levels of attainment – draws authenticity and legitimacy from neuroscience. At the same time, the obsession with producing data on progress re-inscribes a view of ability as fixed and measurable. These ideas produce a form of meritocracy specific to the UK at this particular time: where ability is seen as both fixed *and* influenced by background. I return to these developments in Chapters 4 and 5.

## Merit and ability in the postgenomic age

Although the term is debated, the postgenomic age is defined as the era after the sequencing of the human genome in 2003 (Meloni 2017), in consideration of the important political and ethical ramifications of this scientific breakthrough. The postgenomic era is marked by a move from deterministic understandings of the relation between genes and characteristics – where genes decide who we are – to more fluid conceptions of the interaction between genes and environment. Thus postgenomic understandings of the human are based on a different rationality (Meloni 2017) where the focus is on plasticity and the possibility of 'directing' biological life (Mansfield and Guthman 2015). Work on the 'biosocial' within the sociology of education has drawn attention to the importance of how views of intelligence and environment have been affected by epigenetics, the study of how the environment has an impact on how genes are expressed (Youdell and

Lindley 2018). This field brings into question the notion of fixed inherited intelligence, instead focusing on the interaction of genes and the environment. However, as Youdell notes, 'while epigenetic research is engaging with what the environment does to gene expression and the functioning of the body at the molecular level, work on generalised intelligence is heading in the opposite direction' (Youdell 2016, p. 789). There remain, Youdell argues, engagements with the idea that there are associations between social factors such as race and class, and genes, for all the positivity associated with epigenetics. As in the twentieth century, scientific findings can be used in multiple ways to elaborate on how we understand intelligence or ability. There has been a 'resurgence of genetic explanations' of differences in attainment, including the infamous book *The Bell Curve* in the 1990s, and more recently the work of Robert Plomin at Kings' College London (Tomlinson 2016). The writings of Prime Minister Boris Johnson's key aide Dominic Cummings have come under scrutiny for their controversial viewpoints on genetics (Wintour 2013; Mason and Sample 2020), while my own institution has had to address its own complex history of eugenic thinking (UCL 2020). Thus while the postgenomic age may offer positive avenues for thinking differently about what is inherent to each of us, the arguments related to inherited differences remain in circulation, often associated with respected sources. As Freedman and Ferri note, scientific research 'never exists in a vacuum; it is always a cultural production' (2017, p. 2); new developments are merely part of the long-standing history of producing difference: 'Although our tools get more and more sophisticated and finely tuned, the basis of the desire to locate differences remains the same, despite the futility of these projects' (2017, p. 23).

While I discuss in detail the impact of findings from neuroscience specifically on concepts of ability in Chapter 4, it is worth noting here that these sit within broader scientific developments which are claimed to help us better understand human life and potential (Gulson and Webb 2018). These developments can be seen as evidence of Rose's 'molecular biopolitics' (after Foucault) where 'life has become open to politics' through the development of epigenetic interventions (Rose 2007, p. 15, cited in Gulson and Webb 2018, p. 281). Regulation of the population is an inherent part of education and schooling, but what is particularly relevant here is the continuation of the discourses of normalisation and standardisation and measurability, which are inherently related to race and class, as I discuss further in Chapter 3. As mentioned, the school is a place where regulatory and disciplinary power meet, through the operation of the norm.

## A note on ability and dis/ability

One issue I need to address here is the distinction between 'ability' as intelligence (my focus overall) and ability as the construction through which 'disability' is understood. In DisCrit scholarship, the term ability is used (though cautiously and with caveats) alongside whiteness to describe the interlocking oppressions experienced by people of colour with disabilities (Annamma et al 2018). Here 'ability' is a counterpoint to those deemed in deficit, either physically or mentally, through labels such as 'Special Needs' or in UK schools currently, SEND (Special Educational Needs and Disabilities). Various practices of writing these terms as (dis)ability or dis/ability have been critiqued as euphemisms that obscure disability (Annamma et al 2018) though they are also used to recognise the contested nature of disability.

The idea that some children are labelled as SEND through established discourses of norm/other is clearly important in my discussion of ability as intelligence as a spectrum, though I acknowledge that this label cannot be simply understood as placing students in one place on a linear range, given the complex history of ableism in Western societies and the continued marginalisation of this group. Although it is not my main focus, these labels are part of the assemblage of ability and inequality which I discuss here, and the presence of those deemed other through these discourses clearly has an impact on all students. In their discussion of the future of DisCrit, Annamma et al express their hopes that the field will move beyond 'special education issues', arguing that 'DisCrit is less about disability and race being included in a list of oppressed identities and more about understanding how the interdependence of racism and ableism affect all people' (2018, p. 63). Thus the influence here of DisCrit is subtle but important: I use the term ability in the sense of intelligence only, rather than as 'a socially constructed and privileged norm (similar to Whiteness)' (2018, pp. 64–5), but with an awareness that the interlocking oppressions of dis/ability and race (and indeed class and gender) have a reinforcing effect on broader discourses of 'ability'.

## Current discourses of ability in education

As discussed, there has historically been a certain convenient slipperiness to the terms 'intelligence' and 'ability': in this section, I discuss how this confusion of ideas continues to operate under the umbrella term of ability, using empirical data collected as part of a research project on grouping. I am arguing here that ability as an idea has grown in strength in recent years, while remaining elusive and ill-defined. This is perhaps paradoxical, but as I discuss later, it is the very malleability of ability as a term which allows it to dominate ways of thinking about what children can be within the current *episteme*.

The current use of ability in schools has been described as having three components:

- generalised (the 'able' are assumed to be superior in all high status curricular areas);
- measurable (it is assumed that 'ability' is uniform and easily quantified in teacher assessments and written tests); and
- relatively fixed (those judged as either 'gifted' or 'less able' at an early age are assumed to be destined to remain so throughout their school careers). (Gillborn 2010, p. 245)

Further analysis of 'ability in use', that is the operation of the term within actual schools rather than in policy, is provided by Ladwig and McPherson's (2017) study of Australian primary and secondary teachers' use of the term. They argue that we need to understand the 'internal anatomy' of ability in order to understand 'its capacity to survive' (2017, p. 344). Their data, collected in 2007, demonstrates that use of ability is governed by a 'truly economic rationality', and that it serves the political economic purposes of schooling: 'deciding who gets what from whom, when, where, etc.' (after Foucault) (2017, p. 350). For them, 'the basic structure of the concept of ability in-use is quite simple and is at odds with definitions typically articulated in scholarly reflections on, or defences of, the concept' (2017, p. 345). They identify various aspects of the term from their research data, which I summarise here:

- Ranking: ability allows the comparison of students;
- Internalisation: seeing ability as innate – 'the propensity for the concept of "ability" to be assigned to individual bodies, and the presumption that it is innate to students' (2017, p. 352), as seen in terms such as bright or smart;
- Stabilising: where ability is 'ostensibly stable over time and across contexts within individuals' (2017, p. 353), as seen in a teacher respondent who says they 'can't turn sows ears into silk purses' but can 'get good results if I've good material to work with' (2017, p. 353);
- Externalising: seeing attainment as students' responsibility – 'achievements are understood in almost purely meritocratic terms, i.e. due to their own capacity and effort (2017, p. 354);
- Moralising: including the idea that the 'lower end' are lazy.

The Australian teachers in this study operationalise the idea of fixed and stable intelligence extensively: they comment on the need to be 'realistic' about students' prospects, though this framing is used more with 'lower ability' students (while 'higher ability' students are referred to in terms of extending and potential). As such, the focus is on what students *cannot and never will* do such as 'deeper thinking'. In conclusion, Ladwig and McPherson argue that 'the dominant views of ability that circulate within schools have not broken free of the historical views of intelligence based on biology and heredity, at least in the northern hemisphere' (Ladwig and McPherson 2017, p. 346).

In England, discussions of ability focused on the permanent nature of how ability is understood, in what is called 'fixed ability thinking', are similarly pessimistic: they describe 'a system predicated on testing, "ability"-labelling and grouping, and deficit models of children, [which] routinely fails large numbers of those it is supposed to serve' (Drummond and Yarker 2013). The concept of genetic intelligence is described as the 'zombie theory' that refuses to die, as schools still operate based on this premise despite the lack of scientific evidence (Wrigley 2019).

Building on the findings from teachers in the late 2000s discussed earlier, a further insight into the current use of ability can be gained by my own research data, namely the responses of over 1,000 teachers[1] to the question: 'How do you understand the term "ability" in this context?' on the survey used in the Grouping in Early Years and Key Stage 1 project. By analysing these free text responses – usually one sentence or a few words each but totalling over 15,000 words – we can see how teachers, when pushed for a quick response, describe this concept. I have categorised these responses into 12 different ways of describing ability that were evident in these responses, arranged under three broad headings: ways of thinking about ability as something innate; as a position; and as something child may possess. There is obviously some overlap, and this section ends with an attempt to map out these ideas and show their interrelations.

### Ways of describing ability: as innate

#### Ability as intelligence, skills or talents

I begin this taxonomy of ability with the descriptions which one might perhaps expect, given the history of the term related earlier. Many respondents described ability as 'intelligence' or 'cognitive ability', in line with scientific discourses of different brains operating at different speeds or levels (White 2006). One respondent elucidated what this might mean: "quickness of mind, application, recording skills, memory skills".

This is the simplest conception of ability as innate – that it is something people have inherently to varying degrees. One respondent put simply "Clevers together, thickos together", hopefully ironically. These responses reflect the idea that we can boil down someone's level of intelligence to a single label, though of course the labels vary in acceptability over time (Ball 2013). In several cases, the description reused the term ability, but on a tripartite structure of low/middle/high rather than on a more complex scale, reflecting a division represented on planning sheets:

'More able, able and lower able.'

'More able, middle and less able. Usually focusing on maths and literacy although children may be in different ability groups for each.'

'More able, able, less able & SEND.'

In my view these divisions are different from those related to expectations, discussed later, in that they are labels which are not determined by policy expectations *but by an innate ability*. These are the terms that encompass all areas of the curriculum, and are used to define children as a whole in relation to a norm (though in the case of SEND, policy has a role in terminology). Here we can see Galton's view of a 'general intelligence' (Chitty 2011).

A further set of responses were based on the idea that ability is what some children can do – literally what they are 'able' to accomplish. For example:

'What the children are able to do.'

'What the children can and can't do.'

'Ability to take on information and be able to apply it.'

In this last quote, the implication is that the key ability is absorption of information and application of it. A further variation of this was the idea that some children had talents, which determined their ability:

'Ability is a talent or a skill, their potential to do something and how capable a child is.'

'Ability is the when a child has a talent or finds an area of the curriculum or learning easier than others – whether it be quick to understand mathematical concepts, be artistic, be creative, remember facts, to focus, be well coordinated, be able to cooperate well with others, socialise, read, listening etc. Every child has an ability to do something well.'

These responses reflect the idea that everyone has talents in some way, though what is missing from this point is that the different talents listed are not judged equally valuable by society or indeed schools. There is a certain useful ambiguity in the term 'talents', a comforting idea that we can all be good at something, but also some people are very good at some things, like art or music. Just like the line in the Conservative manifesto quoted in the previous chapter: 'Talent and genius are uniformly distributed throughout the country' (Conservative Party 2019, p. 2), these quotes use 'talents' to mean a number of different areas which a child might be innately good at, creating a softer, more evenly distributed idea of who is 'able'.

### *Ability as potential*

A variant on the 'ability as innate' idea relates to the concept of potential. Here the distance each child can travel is innate (and thus limited), but they may not make use of this. There is some agency on the part of the child, whose path is not determined by their intelligence alone but also by their effort, much as in the intelligence + effort = merit equation. Examples included:

> 'Ability means the best work a child can produce if they are working to their full potential.'

> 'Level of potential attainment.'

> 'A child's potential to achieve a particular aspect of learning.'

Together, these forms of *ability as innate* reproduce the pseudo-scientific discourse of intelligence as something natural, inherent and fixed, which prescribes the limits of what a child can do and classifies them in comparison with others – very much the 'Galtonian thought-world' that White (2006) describes.

## Ways of describing ability: as positional

### *Ability as a set point*

Many respondents described ability in terms of a child occupying a particular point on a spectrum or scale, or a level or phase they can be placed within. Examples include:

> 'Where a child is.'

> 'At a similar point of development or understanding.'

'A sliding scale where peers are compared to teach other, with the highest achievers at the top and SEND learners at the bottom.'

'The level the children are working at.'

'Phase they are secure at.'

'In EYFS [Early Years Foundation Stage] it is developmental level.'

'Level children are at in relation to year group expectations.'

For some, this language of locating a child draws on policy texts (for example development level within the EYFS), while others use analogies such as a sliding scale of comparison, or simply 'where a child is'. This idea of ability is based on two key assumptions: first, that there is an established scale which we can agree on, and second, that the teacher is able to assess it accurately. These ideas are long established in schools and reinforced by policies of teacher assessment (for example, in the EYFS Profile). There is some overlap, clearly, with the high/middle/low descriptions described earlier, but these positions are not necessarily born out of innate differences. Notably, these descriptions do not make a judgement on the child's future or potential, but instead place them on a continuum and compare them with others. It is perhaps then a neutral-sounding way of thinking about ability.

### *Ability as attainment*

One of the simplest ways of describing ability was to describe it as attainment or scores, thereby conflating these two ideas. For example:

'Performance in that particular subject.'

'Based on assessment scores or teacher assessment.'

'In my class it is how good they are at maths and literacy, based on a baseline assessment carried out by head of EYFS (not necessarily the teacher).'

For these teachers, ability is defined by scores, though there may be doubts, as in this last quote, about how these scores are produced. This description, like the idea of ability as a set point discussed earlier, is based on the veracity of assessment and an agreed scale. Here, data are key to shaping how we understand a child, who becomes a 'data double' (Williamson 2014).

### *Ability in relation to a norm*

Several used three-way divisions based on the national average or 'age related expectations' as the norm, with some above and some below, as established in policy, to allocate children:

> 'Whether they are working at age-related expectations, higher or below.'

> 'Whether a child is at ARE [Age Related Expectation] above or below.'

> 'If children are working at, above or below the national average.'

> 'Low ability (working towards the expected standard). Middle ability (working at the expected standard). High ability (working at greater depth).'

Similarly, some early years teachers used the equivalent emerging/expected/exceeding labels used in the EYFS Profile assessment: "Ability is whether children are working towards attaining a concept, have a good understanding of a concept or have mastered a concept. (Emerging, expected or exceeding to use EYFS terms)." Here we see the power of the norm to demarcate those deemed acceptable from those not; this is a simplification of the ability as a set point on a spectrum idea described earlier, where a line is drawn between those below and those above. This is an example of how the 'norm, and its intertwined moral and statistical applications' provide 'a scientific basis for ... measurement and judgement' (Ball 2013, p. 61). The norm – be it ARE or 'expected' on the Profile – appears neutral and common-sense, scientific even, although it is a construct. The tripartite division in some examples also reflects the high/middle/low split seen in the previous section, suggesting a wider tendency to categorise into these three groups.

## Ways of describing ability as something some children possess

### *Ability as readiness*

A further group of responses described ability as having a number of attributes which were not necessarily innate or fixed, though these were fewer in number. One of these was 'readiness', which suggests a position of willingness on the part of the child, separate from structures of levels and comparison with others. Examples included:

> 'Readiness to assimilate new information and build on previous knowledge.'

'Readiness for different degrees of learning.'

'Readiness to learn phonics.'

'The child is ready to understand the concept being taught enabling them to then use and apply it in different contexts.'

The young age of the children taught by these teachers (3–7 years), and the increased frequency of the term 'school readiness' in policy discussion in recent years (Graue 2006; Whitebread and Bingham 2012; Neaum 2016) are probably key factors in the use of this term. The idea that some children arrive at school 'ready to learn', while others do not, is based on discourses of appropriate parenting and neglect which are classed and racialised (Gillies et al 2017). Here the idea of readiness is an individual trait, which allows children to gain from their school experience ('assimilate new information') and learn, and the social implications of readiness are absent (see later for ability as social position). Again, readiness is something that can be assessed by the teacher, but here there is not necessarily a scale or comparison beyond ready or not ready. There are also hints here, however, of a sequential concept of learning where each child has to be secure in what they know before they are 'ready' to move on to the next phase: "I understand it to mean children that need the same or a similar next step. This could be different for each subject and could even be different in each lesson within a subject, depending on the child's prior learning and understanding." This idea has more similarity to the 'ability as positional' points described earlier, as children require different next steps.

### Ability as knowledge

A different form of ability as attribute was evident in responses which focused on knowledge. Here what a child knows determines their ability, which again is not an inherent trait but something acquired. For example, responses included:

'The level of knowledge and understanding.'

'Knowledge of how to apply phonics.'

'Academic knowledge.'

'How much a child knows and how well they can apply that knowledge.'

Here 'knowledge' in both broad and specific forms, and sometimes linked to understanding and application, constitutes ability. This perhaps has links to government rhetoric around the 'knowledge-based curriculum' during the 2010s, as the revised National Curriculum put more emphasis on knowledge (DfE 2017a). Basing 'ability' on knowledge makes more sense if knowledge is the key to success in tests, rather than skills.

### Ability as background

A further and related aspect was the idea that how children are assessed in terms of ability is dependent on background. As these were survey responses the tone of these responses is not clear (particularly whether they approved or disapproved of this link), but the small number of comments which referred to background and family appeared to engage in deficit discourses about some groups of children.

> 'Some children get more support at home. Some children need more help with language skills and are not yet ready for more formal activities.'

> 'Mostly at this age "ability" is tied to age and family input.'

> 'Combination of good language skills, parent support at home, good listening skills.'

This link between support and input at home, and how 'able' children are seen has clear links with the readiness and knowledge discourses discussed earlier; children's ability is seen as based on their experiences at home (Reay 2017). Relatedly, another respondent commented that this 'exposure' to life experiences affects children's ability to grasp new ideas: "To be able to grasp the concept being taught, related to the LO [learning objective]. But depending on life experience, exposure so far to things this varies hugely." As we see in the following chapters, the idea that life experiences affect children's ability is part of a wider, long-established discourse around parenting and class.

### Further aspects of ability as an attribute

There were also several comments which included reference to independence, or what children can do without any adult assistance, using this as a definition for what they could authentically achieve. For example:

> 'Ability to access the learning objective independently.'

> 'What the child can do without excessive adult input.'

These ways of understanding ability as an attribute are distinct from the innate explanations, which suggest a natural inevitability to ability. Instead, these 'ability as attributes' descriptions suggest that children's external environment or how independent they have become are key factors.

### Combinations of different perspectives

To summarise, the main perspectives on ability can be sorted into three broad categories, as shown in Table 2.1:

**Table 2.1**: Perspectives on ability

| Innate | Positional | Attribute |
|---|---|---|
| intelligence, skills or talents | a set point | readiness |
| potential | attainment | knowledge |
| | relation to a norm | background |

This division of the different conceptions of ability into three parts – as innate, as positional and as an attribute – is clearly a simplification of the vast range of different ways of using the term. Later I detail some other descriptions and comments from respondents who sought to challenge the use of the term. However, in the following chapters, we will see how these different conceptions of ability are (re)invigorated in different ways by new developments in education. Here the slipperiness of ability becomes important in allowing the term to operate in evolving and unequal ways.

Before moving on to alternatives outside these three broad categories, I want to emphasise that they were sometimes used together; thus this is a distinction based in my analysis, rather than the representation of conflicting views of ability in operation. For instance:

> 'In this context I understand the term "ability" to mean how well a child is attaining and progressing within a specific area of their learning.'

> 'Where the child is currently working at and speed of absorbing knowledge as well as level of confidence and independence.'

> 'Their level of achievement they are at as well as their capability to achieve.'

> 'Children's intellectual understanding, ability to concentrate, and their grasp of the subject.'

In these comments, ability is simultaneously something innate, something children can demonstrate, knowledge, attainment, speed, confidence and independence. There seem to be no contradictions between these different views, suggesting that ability is a loosely defined and malleable concept. I would argue that these combinations of different ways of understanding the term show that this loose definition is an important feature in its operation – much like the confusion between ability and development I found in early years classrooms (Bradbury 2013b).

One point to consider further here is the falseness of the distinction between ability as positional and ability as innate. These can be used together, as Foucault suggested:

> the regime of disciplinary power … differentiates individuals from one another … it measures in quantitative terms and hierarchizes in terms of value the abilities, the level, the 'nature' of individuals … it traces the limit that will define difference in relation to all other differences, the external frontier of the abnormal. (Foucault 1977, pp. 182–3)

For some, where a child is placed in comparison is a representation of their innate abilities; thus one implies the other. However, when describing children's levels, or placing them in relation to age-related expectations, we cannot assume that there is something innate behind this. I discuss this further in Chapter 5 on datafication.

The three broad categories I set out here – with the first two being more prominent in teachers' responses – show the confusion and 'slipperiness' of the term, but also how this does not prevent its use as a justification for practice. In later chapters I examine how the ideas of ability as innate and ability as positional are reinvigorated by educational developments, and how the idea of ability as attribute relates to these.

## Alternatives and challenges

Within the set of responses to this question there were some exceptional answers. Notably, two participants simply regarded ability as based on phonics alone, responding: "Extent of phonic awareness" and "Ability to decode". Here ability is represented by one particular skill of phonic decoding, perhaps due to the emphasis on the Phonics Screening Check in Year 1 (Bradbury 2018b). Another survey respondent commented that the phonics scheme their school used worked to define ability: "The way in which 'ability' is defined in my school is through the Read Write Inc assessment scheme." This far more limited conception of ability has some commonalities with *ability as skill* and *ability as positional* discussed earlier, but the focus entirely on one skill, and the implicit disapproval of this in the final comment, demarcate these descriptions from others. Here an external system brought in by the school operates to determine ability levels and position. In other comments, although there was mention of maths and literacy as dominant subjects for the assessment of ability, no other specific skill was mentioned, adding to the broader findings of the Grouping Project on the dominance of phonics in early years at least (Bradbury 2018b).

A further set of distinct responses came from those who sought to question and challenge the fixedness or hierarchical nature of ability. For example:

> 'The standard they are working at but we all know that this isn't "set" i.e. they could be greater depth with shape work in Maths but not understand place value so abilities should be looked at per strand/area and not per subject.'
>
> 'It can be counter productive when children and parents see it as hierarchical.'

Both the main categories of ability as positional and ability as innate are challenged here. Others sought to question the measurement of ability:

> 'Based on a very narrow assessment of how quickly children can show in their books or say that they understand. All based on maths and English. It should not be called ability but pace. I call them Pace Groups because they work and understand at different paces. It is disgusting to label someone as "low ability" at the age of 4. Maybe they can't spell but who cares? It just damages their confidence and lets them down.'
>
> 'Ability to produce required evidence (test) at required time to gain score by which ones ability is tested and judged in a limited and unrealistic situation.'

These comments tie into the more generalised doubts about accurate assessment of young children (Ward 2018). Together, these comments represent a challenge to the unquestioned nature of ability and our methods of measuring it; they serve as an important reminder that we cannot assume that teachers continue blindly following usual practices without thinking through their implications. Moreover, they also remind us that the links between teachers' beliefs and the classroom practices they perpetuate are complex (Marks 2013; Bradbury 2019e; Braun and Maguire 2020).

## The implications of ability

Having mapped out the different conceptions of ability as demonstrated in the survey responses, in this section I focus on the implications of ability in classrooms; that is, the way in which these discourses determine what happens to children in schools. These different ways of describing ability operate as regimes of truth which *classify*, *distribute* and *exclude* (Gore 1995). This section mainly focuses on the organisational impact in terms of grouping and interventions (where children are removed from the main classroom for a period), though there are far more subtle ways in which ability affects interactions between teacher and pupil and between pupils, as discussed in later sections.

### Grouping practices

There is an extensive literature on grouping by 'ability' and attainment, its forms and effects, from school systems around the world (Ireson and Hallam 2001; Campbell 2013; Marks 2016; Francis et al 2019; McGillicuddy and Devine 2018, 2020; Towers et al 2020). Underlying these practices are the two main principles about ability identified earlier: that it is fixed and innate, and that it can be measured and used to compare students. Grouping takes many different forms, however, and these are always contingent on within-school factors, such as staffing, facilities, and numbers of pupils; and external factors, such as the policy context and the educational philosophies of the time (producing a shift, for example, between comprehensive educational ideals and competitive visions of success (Gewirtz 2002)).

To be clear on the use of these terms, the main forms of grouping usually identified in operation in primary and secondary schools are as follows:

- **Streaming:** when children are placed in a class, usually for the entire year, based on a general view of their ability across the curriculum. This is rarely used in primary schools.
- **Setting:** when children are placed in classes for particular subjects, mainly literacy and maths, and move from their normal class for this subject.

- **(Within–class) Ability grouping:** where ability groups are used within a class, usually sat at different tables with different tasks and levels of support. This may occur in a mixed-ability class, or indeed within a set. This form is more common in primary schools (adapted from Bradbury 2018b).

These variations may be used together, for example in secondary schools which stream pupils for the year, and then organise sets within the streams. The degree of movement between sets and streams also varies between schools and may be based on teacher judgement or attainment data (Francis et al 2019; Neumann 2021).

In addition to these usual forms of grouping practice, I have added a fourth variant (Bradbury 2018b):

- **Interventions:** when specific children are targeted and removed from the class at regular times for additional support or extension activities; this is often for a fixed period of time and a specific purpose, such as booster groups used before assessments.

This is not a system of general classroom organisation, but an ongoing and often temporary separation of one group of pupils from the rest of their peers, on the basis of attainment or ability. Interventions are usually used in primary schools to address a particular skill – such as reading or phonic decoding – or to improve the attainment of a targeted group. This group is removed from the classroom to work with a teacher or teaching assistant in another area for a period of the day, thus missing what is happening in the main classroom. They may be a borderline group in a form of educational triage (Gillborn and Youdell 2000; Marks 2014), where resources are allocated based on who will best improve the overall attainment results, but not necessarily so. Some intervention groups are based on 'catching up' children who are seen as falling behind, or more rarely, for 'gifted and talented' pupils (Bradbury 2018b). There are also one-to-one systems of interventions where a member of staff works intensively for a short period with one child.

I argue that interventions should be taken into account in discussions of grouping practices because although they are short term and relate to only one group of pupils, they represent the same sets of values and principles as other grouping practices. That is, interventions are based on the idea that *we can know who needs something different*, and the physical placement of children can be based on this. Interventions are in some ways a more brutal form of the 'bottom group' or 'bottom set', often demarcating the 'abnormal' from the normal (although not always so, but they are frequently seen as aimed at lower-attaining children). There can be negative effects of interventions, such as a narrowed curriculum (Dunne et al 2011) or being taught by less qualified staff in inappropriate teaching spaces (Brown 2017).

In the Grouping Project the teachers explained their grouping systems using both practical and educational reasons: "I personally think it's better for the children because otherwise your more able children get bored and frustrated, your less able children just get left behind. So the grouping means that you can focus your attention" (School Leader, Whiteread Primary). Here there is a need to group children because otherwise behaviour will be affected, and some children will not be able to access the learning and become 'left behind'. Overall the teachers in the Grouping Project were unquestioning in their use of ability differences as a justification for the physical organisation of pupils though grouping or interventions – the current 'practices of division' (Foucault 1982) in schools. This does not mean that they approved of grouping, however, but in a context of intense pressure arising from policy reform, they saw it as a 'necessary evil' (Bradbury and Roberts-Holmes 2017b).

Interventions also had a particular role as evidence that children's attainment had been monitored and there was some response on the school's part to children who were not making adequate progress. In this case, a teacher explained how 'pupil progress meetings', where the class teacher sits down to discuss the data with a senior teacher, became a system which produced further interventions:

> 'I used to enjoy my pupil progress meetings when we used to talk about the children. Now you come in, all your data in your hands and literally we get names reeled off, these are the children who are not on track on a thingy, "I want to know what you're doing". It literally is a list of interventions, any intervention. There's no thought. You don't talk about the child, it's just occasionally even said in meetings and again. I don't blame them for this because they're panicking: "Even if you think it's not going to have an impact, we have to have something on this bit of paper so that when it doesn't, we can show that we at least did something". It's like a parallel universe.' (Focus Group 2 Teacher)

Here, the pressure from Ofsted means that 'any intervention' is needed to demonstrate that the data have been considered and practice has been altered in response. This 'parallel universe' of organising interventions based on data about who is 'not on track' uses a discourse of *ability as positional* to allocate children to additional sessions.

In a further research study on the impact of statutory tests (SATs) in the final year of primary school, headteachers of primary schools similarly explained why grouping was necessary in preparation for high stakes tests (Bradbury 2019d). Interventions, in particular, were used to 'fill in gaps' and support those on the 'cusp' of reaching expected levels: "probably three afternoons there's maths intervention. With a qualified teacher … it depends who we think could benefit. If they're cuspy, both top and bottom probably. So, the higher ability probably get some and then the cuspy ones get some" (Headteacher, School F). Here the 'high ability' children get additional maths on three afternoons, perhaps so that they achieve the 'greater depth' benchmark in their SATs, as well as the 'cuspy' children, who might attain the main benchmark. This is a system of educational triage, where the children on the cusp of achieving the benchmark are prioritised (Gillborn and Youdell 2000). There was also evidence of the power of ability as a concept in one school which operated a system of higher, middle and lower classes through the school (streaming); in this school, the children's whole day – who they interacted with, their teacher, the curriculum – was affected by whether they had been labelled high, middle or lower ability.

Despite these concerns about the impact on pupils, many teachers still see grouping as necessary in the current policy context (Bibby et al 2017; Bradbury 2018b). In these examples from research projects, we see how 'pedagogy proceeds via classificatory mechanisms – the classification of knowledge, the ranking and classification of individuals and groups' (Gore 1995, p. 174). There is also *normalisation* – the differentiation of individuals from and each other – in the distinction made between those 'on track' and those not, and those 'cuspy' and not, which results in the micropractice of power of *distribution* and *exclusion*, in their allocation to intervention groups. This is disciplinary power working on bodies within the classroom, through teachers' engagement with ideas about ability.

Importantly, grouping systems are both a manifestation of, and productive of, discourses of ability. As Archer et al comment, 'set allocation is seen as a reflection of "natural" differences in "ability" between students' (2018, p. 122); placement in particular groups becomes evidence of innate and measurable fixed differences in ability. At the same time, the different work set and completed, or the different patterns of behaviour among groups, become further evidence of differences between pupils.

## Interactions between teacher and pupil

Research has suggested that teachers' perceptions of children's ability affects their interactions with them, often reproducing the same position within a hierarchy of children. Marks' (2016) observational work on primary grouping identified the quite clear ways in which a teacher might respond differently to those children that they see as 'high ability': different questioning, praise, the 'benefit of the doubt' when work is incorrect or incomplete. Similarly, a teacher's interaction with a 'low ability' pupil can also be affected by this label, lowering expectations and perhaps blinding them to what a child can achieve.

In my own ethnographic research in Reception classrooms of 4–5 year olds, I found learner identities were built up very quickly in the children's first few weeks of school, and these affected all aspects of classroom life for children (Bradbury 2013b). Those seen as 'high ability' were encouraged to try different activities, asked more challenging questions and allowed greater flexibility in terms of conduct and behaviour. Children seen as 'lower ability' were allowed to fixate on one activity during free play sessions, while also being criticised for their lack of effort. Some children had arrived at the school already labelled by their nursery teacher as H, M or L – high, middle or low ability – in the handover meeting with their new teacher; this in turn influenced how they were perceived from the very first meeting. Furthermore, Yarker argues that ' "Fixed-ability" thinking isn't so much a policy as a way of life in the school system' (2019, p. 3), citing undergraduates' reflections on how the ways in which they were labelled in terms of ability affected their school experiences, although they had never previously regarded 'ability' as a questionable concept.

The research on interactions demonstrates that ability does not merely function as a principle of organising, but is inflected in every conversation between child and teacher; thus we must consider the 'hidden micro-mechanisms of its operation' (Tamboukou 2003, p. 140, cited in Ball 2013, p. 37) as well as the broader discourses.

## Children's identities as learners

Perceptions of ability are a key part of a child's identity as a learner, as perceived by the teacher, along with behaviour and attitude to learning. Ability also forms a key part of how a child views themselves, importantly. Teachers in the Grouping Project described their concern that children's self-esteem would be affected by grouping; as one respondent commented, "I do think it can really damage self-esteem – the children who spend their whole education in the bottom group." A participant in one of the focus groups told a story of how one girl's aspiration to be a doctor like her mother disappeared when she was moved down a set:

> 'She said, "I used to want to be a doctor like my mum but since I moved to the middle set I've realised that that's not something I can do, because I'm not good enough so I'm thinking about what else I might do in the future."' (Focus Group 2 participant)

We see here the emotional injury that ability grouping can have upon children's identities as learners and their future aspirations.

Hargreaves et al's (2021) study of children in 'low ability' groups echoes these teachers' concerns: the children they spoke to who were placed in 'lower' groups came to feel 'socially isolated and powerless', placed away from friends, bored and frustrated. They thought the teacher chose them to answer questions less often and they feared bullying. For some, behaviour was in turn affected by their low group placement, as some children chose means of 'subtle resistance'. Scherer's (2016) study in primary schools showed that young children may react in violent or disruptive ways to being labelled, to 'avoid the stigma of being positioned at the bottom of the heap'. Grouping has a huge impact on children's view of themselves; it 'acts as a psychosocial filter influencing how children know, feel and are as learners' (McGillicuddy and Devine 2020, p. 564).

These findings in primary schools echo Reay's argument, based on secondary school research, that 'When we expect to be viewed as inferior our abilities seem to be diminished, and this sense of inferiority is particularly strong in the bottom sets' (Reay 2017, p. 77). Similarly in their study of secondary pupils, Francis et al (2020) found significant differences in the self-confidence scores of pupils in top and bottom sets, which accumulated over time. Furthermore the responses of students interviewed for the study showed how young people 'can internalize and reproduce the cultural arbitrary through the view that set positions are allocated on the basis of academic and behavioural personal merit' (Archer et al 2018, p. 130); students believed themselves to be of higher or lower ability because they were placed there. Students in top sets were 'proud', while those in lower sets were 'embarrassed' and stigmatised. Reay describes a 'sense of abjection and failure' for those in the 'bottom set' (2017, p. 70). This is a major implication of the discourse of ability.

## Conclusion

The discussion in this chapter has moved from unearthing some of the origins of concepts of intelligence and ability, to categorising how teachers currently use the term, to how it affects what happens in schools. There is no doubt, looking at the research findings here, that ability operates powerfully as an underlying principle in schools, affecting classroom practice – what we might see as its disciplinary function, producing labelling, hierarchy, and *classification* and *exclusion* (Gore 1995). This operation is affected, however, by the regulatory power of ability, which is drawn from the pseudo-scientific origins of eugenics and intelligence testing, and which has been given new impetus for some by developments in genetics. As Baker has argued, the 'new eugenics' can be seen in the 'the everyday dividing, sorting and classifying practices of schooling', which relate ultimately to the ' "quality control" of national populations' (2002 cited in Gillborn 2008, p. 114). This biopolitical discourse – where we can maximise benefit by understanding how to develop everyone's talents – reinforces the everyday mechanisms of ability in schools. This is discussed further in the following chapter. This chapter has emphasised that there is still 'the need to dismantle all the structures rooted in the fallacy of fixed ability or potential' (Chitty 2011, p. 245), at all levels.

The descriptions of ability discussed in this chapter provide a framework for understanding the following chapters on educational trends. Discourses of *ability as innate* conceive of ability in biological, or more specifically neurological, terms: ability is something hard-wired into children, physically present in their brains to varying degrees. In contrast, the descriptions of ability as a placement on a spectrum, or in relation to a norm, focus on the *measurability* of ability, though these scores and positions may be seen as representations of something innate of course. This *ability as positional* discourse represents a simplification of complexity, with a focus on comparison against norms and standards. I argue here that relating to these two ways of talking of ability there are two powerful developments or trends in education: the influence of neuroscience, and the increasing reliance on data. The threads of these two ideas, which both reinforce and are reinforced by these educational trends, can be identified historically, but it is only through an analysis of their contemporary relevance that we can begin to unravel their unequal impact on students.

# 3

# How does the idea of ability relate to inequalities?

## Introduction

This chapter begins by setting out the extent and nature of inequalities in the education system in England, based on attainment data. Then, using research data from interviews with teachers, I set out the case for the argument that 'ability' and inequality are intertwined concepts, reinvigorated by recent developments. The literature discussed in the later part of the chapter demonstrates that the notion of ability has always been inflected with raced and classed discourses, but I argue here that the idea has been reinvigorated so that it works in new ways in the current system, and the post-pandemic era offers new dangers, as well as new ways of thinking.

As mentioned, I use the term inequalities[1] here to consider those disparities relating mainly to class and race. The intention is not to dismiss other forms of inequality, but simply to make the topic manageable. Other scholars have dealt more thoroughly with issues of gender, religion, sexuality, dis/ability and others, and their intersection; and how this relates to perceptions of ability and students' identities as learners (Francis and Skelton 2005; Jackson 2006; Walkerdine and Ringrose 2006; Bradford and Hey 2007; Skelton et al 2007; Shain 2010; Slee 2011; Youdell 2011; Mirza and Meetoo 2018). I focus on class and race because (along with gender) these are major organising principles in education, which have been associated with differing levels of intelligence historically.

## Educational inequalities

In this section I draw on attainment and exclusion data from England in order to consider the current state of educational inequalities. This is by no means an exhaustive catalogue of the multiple ways in which the education system divides and classifies within hierarchies of success, but through the use of published statistics we can at least recognise which students come out of the education system with the means to continue in education, and with the markers of educational 'success' which open up opportunities. This exploration is based on the logic that in order to see the effect of 'ability' as a concept on inequality, we need to see who benefits. To elaborate further, Scheurich argues (drawing on Foucault) that: 'there are powerful "grids" or networks of regularities ... that are constitutive of the emergence or social construction of a particular problem as a social problem' (Scheurich 1994, p. 301).

Thus, to understand how policy comes to define a problem and solution, we must begin to unravel the *regularities* that govern their constitution as such. I would argue that ability is one such regularity: it forms the basis of much thinking about how education should function, and therefore what is understood as a problem. For example, the annual concern over rising grades and gender differences in attainment is rooted in the idea that ability is innate (and therefore rising grades are indicative of easier exams, not cleverer students; boys are unfairly penalised by inappropriate assessments).

So, where do we locate responsibility for these regularities, or for the dominant discourses that operate as *regimes of truth* in education? Scheurich argues that 'regularities are not intentional; that is, no particular individual or group consciously created them'; however, 'this does not mean that no individual or group may not benefit from the regularities' (1994, p. 301). Similarly, scholars using CRT describe the lack of explicit intentionality in the creation of policies which systematically disadvantage minoritised students; as Gillborn says 'this is not a conspiracy; it's worse than that', because iniquitous results are the product of the normal workings of the system which is institutionally racist (2006b). In reference to ability, we could lay the blame with the nineteenth-century scientists who popularised the idea of inheritable intelligence, though we know the idea has far older roots and was always contested (Youdell 2016). It is perhaps more fruitful to instead consider *who gains* from the current system, and who suffers, in line with CRT perspectives on education. In a game where the idea of ability as fixed is present, who wins and who loses? For this reason, I set out over the following pages the educational statistics provided by the government (using their own problematic race labels, collected when children begin school, and other official categories), based on high-stakes tests.[2] These range from assessments undertaken by teachers at age 4–5, to GCSE attainment at the end of secondary school. I also refer to exclusion statistics, all the while bearing in mind that 'assessment is fundamentally a social activity, it is based on social assumptions and carries social consequences' (Stobart 2008, p. 35).

*Attainment in early years*

Attainment in early years (age 0–5) is measured by the Early Years Foundation Stage Profile (EYFSP), an assessment conducted throughout the Reception year of primary school, when children are 4–5 years old. It is based on teacher judgement across the whole curriculum, and the benchmark used by government is named a 'Good Level of Development' or GLD. Overall, 72 per cent of children attained GLD in 2019 – 64 per cent of boys and 78 per cent of girls (UK Government 2019a).

Figure 3.1 shows the proportion of children in each ethnic group[3] attaining GLD in 2019, divided into those eligible for FSM[4] and those not (UK Government 2020a). As well as the clear differences between pupils receiving FSM and their peers, which are present across all groups, there are also clear differences between ethnic groups. There is a gap of over ten percentage points between the highest-attaining non-FSM groups (Indian and Mixed White/Asian) and the lowest (Bangladeshi, Black Other, White Other). Furthermore, the difference between pupils on FSM and not varies per ethnic group: notably, the 'FSM penalty' is greater for White British pupils (who make up the majority of pupils).

**Figure 3.1:** Percentage of children attaining GLD at age 4/5 in England, 2019 by ethnic group and FSM status

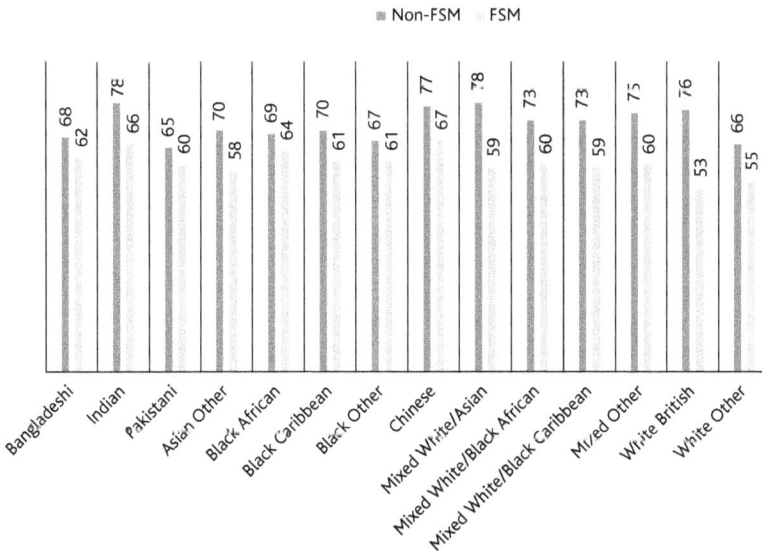

These data need to be understood in context, as based on teacher assessment, which is often influenced by the need to produce a good 'Ofsted story' of low attainment on entry (Bradbury and Roberts-Holmes 2017a). However, they do mark a clear moment of labelling in the child's school career, and indeed ordering, as children are given individual scores. Also, the children are assessed when they have been in school for one year (or sometimes two if they attended a school nursery class), so the use of these data as 'entry' statistics is misleading: these data do not show that the gaps are already there when children arrive, but rather demonstrate that within a short period, disparities in attainment between racialised groups and by social class are well established. These then lay the foundation, and provide a justification, for the inequalities seen in later years.

## Attainment in primary schools

Attainment at age 10/11, at the end of primary education, is assessed through SATs tests in Reading, Mathematics, and Spelling, Punctuation and Grammar (SPaG) and teacher assessments in Writing. Here the benchmark in each subject is known as 'reaching the expected standard', and there is a higher level of attainment recorded, called 'greater depth' or the 'higher standard'. Overall, 65 per cent of children – 60 per cent of boys and 70 per cent of girls (UK Government 2020b) – reached the 'expected standard' in Reading, Writing and Maths, which is the government's published measure, in 2019. Figure 3.2 shows the proportion of children reaching the expected standard in SATs tests by ethnic group and FSM status.

Again, there are stark disparities between those on FSM and not, and between ethnic groups. In the highest-attaining group, the Chinese pupils, 80 per cent of Non-FSM and 75 per cent of FSM pupils reach the expected standard, which is more than the overall totals for most other groups. In some FSM groups, the percentage reaching the expected standard is below 50: this is the case for the Black Caribbean, Mixed White/Black Caribbean, White British and White Other groups. These SATs assessments are used to measure the school's effectiveness overall, but they also have an impact on each pupil's predicted grades at secondary school. Children entering secondary school who did not reach the expected standard may not be expected to reach similar benchmarks at GCSE. Indeed, Taylor-Mullings' research in secondary schools found that 'the judgements made about children's ability at KS2 were fixed and then determined whether they would be in the target group, irrespective of their performance prior to that assessment period

**Figure 3.2:** Percentage of children reaching the expected standard at age 10/11 in England, 2019 by ethnic group and FSM status

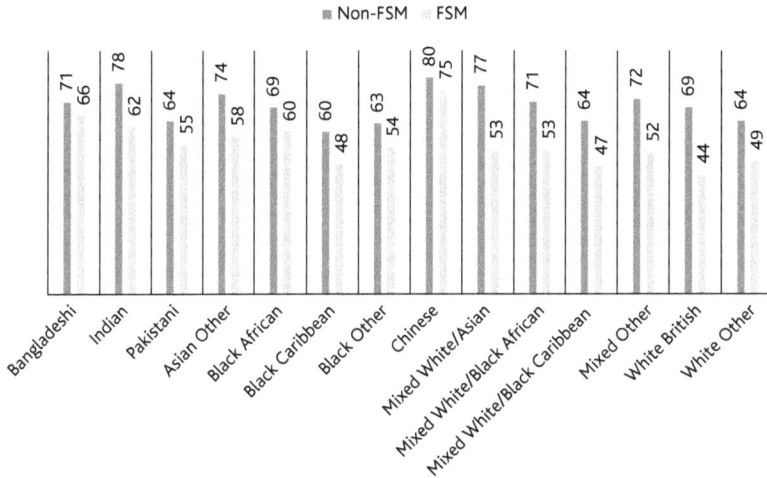

Note: Ethnic group labels are listed here in order of the large groupings used by government: Asian, Black, Chinese, Mixed, White. The White British group is the largest population, with over 400,000 children entered for the EYFSP, while other groups are much smaller: only 3,000 Chinese pupils are represented here.

or at KS3' (2018, p. 274). Moreover, some pupils were deemed to be 'not worth working with' at secondary because they were so unlikely to reach the benchmarks featured in secondary league tables.

At the end of primary school, the FSM penalty is over 20 percentage points in some ethnic groups, including the White British group: it is clear that, caveats about the bluntness of FSM as a tool aside, coming from a disadvantaged family has an impact on your chances of reaching the expected standard.

## Attainment in secondary schools

Attainment in secondary schools is measured through data from GCSE examinations, and compiled in a variety of formats (as I discuss in more detail in Chapter 5). A major benchmark the government uses is the proportion of students getting a Grade 5 (described as a 'strong pass') or above in English and Maths (UK Government 2020c). This was achieved by 43.2 per cent of pupils in England overall in 2019 – 40.0 per cent of boys and 46.6 per cent of girls. For FSM pupils, the figure was 22.5 per cent, and their non-FSM peers, 46.6 per cent. Figure 3.3 shows the percentage of pupils getting Grades 5–9 in English and Maths in England by ethnic group and FSM status.

**Figure 3.3:** Percentage of pupils getting Grades 5–9 in English and Maths in England, 2019 by ethnic group and FSM status

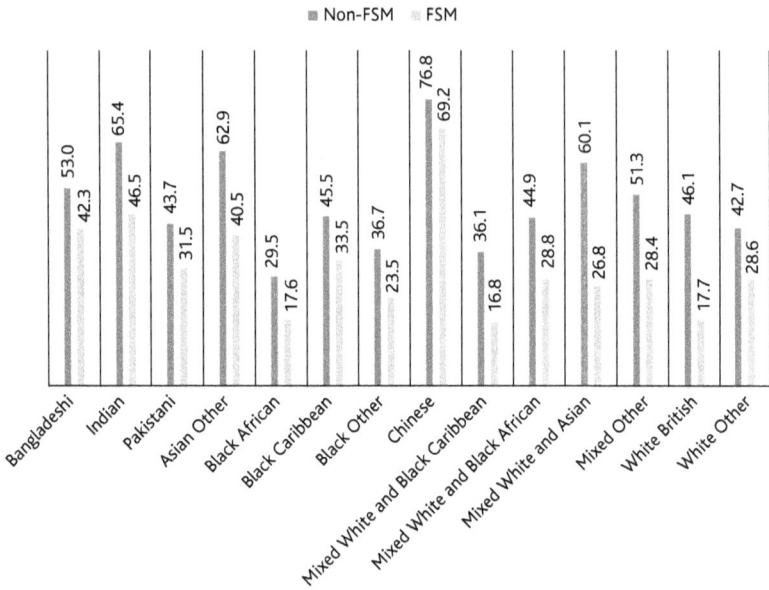

■ Non-FSM  ▪ FSM

| Ethnic group | Non-FSM | FSM |
|---|---|---|
| Bangladeshi | 53.0 | 42.3 |
| Indian | 65.4 | 46.5 |
| Pakistani | 43.7 | 31.5 |
| Asian Other | 62.9 | 40.5 |
| Black African | 29.5 | 17.6 |
| Black Caribbean | 45.5 | 33.5 |
| Black Other | 36.7 | 23.5 |
| Chinese | 76.8 | 69.2 |
| Mixed White and Black Caribbean | 36.1 | 16.8 |
| Mixed White and Black African | 44.9 | 28.8 |
| Mixed White and Asian | 60.1 | 26.8 |
| Mixed Other | 51.3 | 28.4 |
| White British | 46.1 | 17.7 |
| White Other | 42.7 | 28.6 |

These figures, which indicate a basic level of success for secondary students, again show stark disparities between those on FSM and not, and particularly for the White British majority. As discussed later, this has led to calls for policy to concentrate on the 'white working class'. There is also a great deal of variation in the difference within ethnic groups between FSM and not. As Keddie (2015) summarised:

> While poverty (or more accurately, the take up of Free School Meals [FSM] – as a proxy indicator of socio-economic class) is correlated with under-performing students from Black Caribbean, Pakistani and Bangladeshi backgrounds, it is a much more salient predictor of underachievement for the White British population than it is for minority ethnic groups. (2015, p. 518)

There are also distinct differences between ethnic groups, with the percentage between the highest-attaining Chinese group and the Black Caribbean group at over 50 per cent, for both FSM and non-FSM groups.

## Exclusion figures

Exclusion data are an alternative source of information about the experiences of young people from minoritised groups and those on FSM in schools. Temporary (or 'fixed period') exclusion figures, using data from both primary and secondary level, show clear differences by ethnic group. The most up-to-date figures available, from the 2017–18 school year, show an exclusion rate of 5.70 per cent for the White British majority group (UK Government 2019c). Table 3.1 shows the three highest and three lowest rates for the main ethnic groups.[5]

To put these into perspective, this means that for every 10,000 Black Caribbean pupils, there are 1,046 temporary exclusions, but for the same number of Chinese pupils, there are 50. For the White British group, there are 570 fixed period exclusions for every 10,000 pupils. There are also differences in the data by FSM eligibility: the temporary exclusion rate for pupils receiving FSM in the same year was 13.65 per cent, or 1,365 per 10,000 pupils, compared to 3.73 per cent or 373 per 10,000 pupils for non-FSM (UK Government 2019c).

If we look at the figures for the more serious permanent exclusions (Table 3.2), there is a similar pattern. Note that the rate for the White British group is 0.10 per cent, or 10 per 10,000 pupils.

Again, thinking about this per 10,000 pupils, there would be 28 exclusions for the Black Caribbean group, ten for the White British group, and one exclusion for Chinese pupils.[6] The rate of permanent exclusion for pupils with FSM was 0.28 per cent compared to 0.07 per cent for non-FSM (UK Government 2019c).

**Table 3.1:** Temporary exclusion rates of selected ethnic groups, in England, 2017–18

| Lowest rates | | Highest rates | |
| --- | --- | --- | --- |
| Chinese | 0.50% | Black Caribbean group | 10.46% |
| Indian | 0.75% | Mixed White/Black Caribbean | 10.13% |
| Asian Other | 1.45% | Black Other | 5.80% |

**Table 3.2:** Permanent exclusion rates of selected ethnic groups, in England, 2017–18

| Lowest rates | | Highest rates | |
| --- | --- | --- | --- |
| Chinese | 0.01% | Black Caribbean group | 0.28% |
| Indian | 0.02% | Mixed White/Black Caribbean | 0.27% |
| Asian Other | 0.03% | Mixed White/Black African | 0.14% |

These figures have consistently been a source of concern for researchers, campaigners and, to some extent, in policy circles (Youdell 2006; Parsons 2009; Bei in press). A review commissioned in 2018 by the then Secretary of State for Education, Damien Hinds, concluded that there was 'too much variation in exclusion practice' and 'there is more we can do to ensure that every exclusion is lawful, reasonable and fair; and that permanent exclusion is always a last resort' (Timpson 2019, p. 3).

## The frames of debate about education and inequality

So to return to the question raised above, who does gain from the system governed by ability as a regularity, or as a dominant discourse? First, there are clear advantages to being more affluent, or at least not having a level of income which means a child is in receipt of FSM, to be more specific. Pupils in every ethnic group are considerably more likely to attain the government benchmarks if they are in the non-FSM category. Second, the chances of attaining the set standards are higher if you are in certain ethnic groups, notably Chinese, Indian, and Mixed White/Asian. The White British majority not on FSM attain well also, but fewer than half of the White British pupils on FSM reach the expected standard at primary school (44 per cent).

In this section I examine how the data discussed earlier have been understood in political debates and in academic scholarship, before I consider in more detail how they relate to discourses of ability. There is not space here for a thorough account of the scholarship in the field of race and class in education; instead, I point to some key debates which have been prominent in discussions of educational inequality, both in the 2010s and in the era of COVID-19.

### Institutional racism

A major area of debate within discussions of racialised inequalities in education in the last 20 years has been on institutional racism. The term was popularised by the MacPherson Report of 1999 into the police handling of the murder of a Black teenager, Stephen Lawrence (Macpherson 1999). MacPherson's definition gave wider acceptance to a view of racism as part of the everyday workings of the system, rather than as an isolated event; this echoed longer-standing perceptions of racism as endemic and 'business as usual' found in CRT scholarship (Delgado and Stefancic 2000). There was a particular focus on the attainment and experiences of Black students during the 2000s, with David Gillborn's work applying CRT to the system in England (Gillborn 2008) and emphasising the continued inequalities that arise from the 'normal workings' of the education system. My research in primary education found that assumptions about minoritised (and disadvantaged) children in inner city schools meant that pupils were systematically assessed with lower grades at age 4–5 because these were the only assessments that were intelligible for these children (Bradbury 2013b). This was systematic and repeated each year, but unwitting, so that it fitted the definition of institutional racism – or perhaps, as it also involved poorer White children, systematic discrimination.

There were improvements in the attainment of Black children in secondary education in the 2000s and 2010s, but as Taylor-Mullings (2018) contends, these were not the result of policies which were intended to address disparities in attainment. Instead, the education policies of the 'incentivising state', which aimed at overall improvement in GCSE figures, included some Black students, in a case of 'interest convergence'. This is a term from CRT which describes a situation where the interests of the minority and the White majority converge (Bell 1992). Of course, not all Black children benefitted equally: those with low scores at the end of primary education were seen as not worth working on: 'Black children adversely affected by these policies were those considered to have little value to successive governments and schools because they were deemed incapable of attaining the headline performance measure' (Taylor-Mullings 2018, p. 303).

Once these children had been deemed 'low ability' due to their primary SATs results, they were of little value in the accountability-driven system. This echoes Gillborn and Youdell's (2000) earlier findings from the 1990s, where Black pupils and those on FSM were disproportionately allocated to the 'hopeless case' group, deemed not worthy of effort as they would not reach the GCSE benchmark grade.

Looking back over this longer period of a neoliberal education system driven by high-stakes tests, we can see a clear pattern in the attainment of minoritised groups, and Black students in particular, at secondary level. Analysis by Gillborn et al (2017) over a 25-year period shows that although there have been reductions in the attainment gap between Black pupils and their White peers, each time the benchmark measures have been changed, this gap has widened again. Thus, they conclude that 'the negative impacts of policy changes have been much more certain and predictable than occasional attempts to reduce race inequality' (2017, p. 848).

The charge of institutional racism, brought to the fore again by the Black Lives Matter protests in 2020, remains a key question in education. Exclusion statistics remain a key indicator of a system which disproportionately fails Black students, and Black boys in particular (Bei in press). This is a system, Bei contends, which makes Black boys have special educational needs (SEN) status for behaviour, just as Black children were *made* 'Educationally Subnormal' by the school system in Bernard Coard's research in the 1960s and 1970s (Coard 1971). This results in the 'disproportionate spatial and symbolic removal of Black children from mainstream settings into special schools' (Bei in press); this is the 'SENitisation' of minority children found internationally, a collision of discourses based on ableism and racism which work to exclude the educational Other (Migliarini 2018). Thus, although the issue of 'white working class' children in education has become more prominent in public debate, as I discuss later, there remain key questions for education about its role as an institutionally racist sector.

### 'Model minorities'

A further element of the race and education field is the issue of 'model minorities' (Gillborn 2008). The results of the highest-attaining groups – Indian, Mixed White/Asian and Chinese – have resulted in their being described as a 'model minority', in line with the use of the term to refer to Asian-Americans in the US. This term is problematic in several ways: first, it homogenises the groups, who are seen as universally 'hard-working', for example, through often negative stereotypes. Second, it places other minorities as *not* model – there cannot be an ideal without a concomitant pathologisation of the rest (Lee 2008). Third, it allows for the disavowal of racism, in what I have referred to as the 'racist to all or none' argument (Bradbury 2013a). This is the explanation that the system as a whole cannot be racist if some ethnic groups are successful; the nonsensical position that the system must be equally detrimental to all non-white groups or not at all. The 'model minority' discourse also has a particular relationship to discussions about the intelligence of different groups, as although these students are successful, it is seen as having been achieved in the 'wrong way' (Archer and Francis 2007). This delegitimisation of minoritised students' success is achieved through discourses of 'pushy parents', rote learning or overwork, so that their achievement is rendered 'inauthentic' (Archer 2008; Bradbury 2013a). In some cases, this inauthentic success is placed in contrast with an innate high ability (working hard juxtaposed with being intelligent naturally), though in some cases students from the minority group are stereotyped as 'clever' too (Bradbury 2013a). This position of success as a model minority is always precarious; models can be disposable when 'racism plays favourites' (Gillborn 2008, p. 153).

### The focus on the 'white working class'

The publication of attainment statistics, such as those for GCSEs discussed earlier, which show that White British pupils in receipt of FSM are one of the lowest-attaining groups in schools, have driven a concern for the 'white working class' pupils throughout the late 2000s and 2010s (Sveinsson 2009; Strand 2014; Keddie 2015; Travers 2017). Research has attempted to identify reasons for the low attainment of this group: the teachers in Demie and Lewis' study described the main barriers to success as 'lack of parental aspiration and engagement in school life, poverty and inadequate housing stock, marginalisation and perceived loss of culture and language difficulties' (2011, p. 251). For some teachers, the focus on other minority students came at the expense of the white working class (Keddie 2015). However, there has been much criticism of this discourse of the white working class as the 'new victims', as this positions groups in opposition to one another in a zero-sum game, as if only one group could be disadvantaged by the system. It also fails to acknowledge the privileges of whiteness, even for those from poorer backgrounds (Gillborn 2009; Keddie 2015). A further major issue, highlighted by Gillborn (2009), is that pupils on FSM make up approximately 13 per cent of the school population, but 57 per cent of the wider British public describe themselves as 'working class'. Thus, when headlines state that the 'white working class' are the lowest attaining, far more people perceive this as applying to them than accurate. This is the 'construction of white racial victimhood', in Gillborn's words.

The introduction of the Pupil Premium, which is additional for pupils who are or have been on FSM in the last six years, has produced a new label – as we see in the data extracts later in this book. Being 'Pupil Premium' is conflated with being 'disadvantaged', which also has a technical meaning as it includes pupils in local authority care and with SEND, in some cases. The Conservative governments of the 2010s frequently pointed to the closing of the gap between 'disadvantaged pupils' and their peers, using a different definition. During the pandemic, the description of 'vulnerable' children within discussion of the impact of school closures included 'Children living in poverty' (Children's Commissioner 2020). This confusion of terms has perhaps moved the discourse on from the focus on the 'white working class', but as we have seen earlier, there remain serious disparities in terms of class within the education system. It is important to remember that class-based disparities in attainment and experiences have a long history (Reay 2017). The labels of 'Pupil Premium' and 'disadvantaged' are very recent additions to the lexicon of class in education. Extensive research over decades has established that 'For working-class children, classrooms are often places of routine everyday humiliations and slights' (Reay 2017, p. 77), including, of course, being labelled in terms of ability.

Having outlined these issues relating to inequalities in education more broadly, I now return to the interaction with discourses of ability more specifically.

## The interaction of ability with inequality

In this section, I use some research data and wider scholarship to consider how ability interacts with inequalities. A central argument is that ability, as an idea, does a great deal of work in establishing, maintaining and reinforcing patterns of inequality. It is 'a façade that blinds actors to their own roles in creating or reinforcing education and social inequality' (Ladwig and McPherson 2017, p. 348), an ideological construct that has a huge impact. It is problematic, but widely accepted: 'forms of determinism – or "bell curve thinking" – have been normalised in education, most notably in the fallacious view that "intelligence" is distributed in the population according to such a curve' (Drummond and Yarker 2013, p. 6).

Ladwig and McPherson argue that 'a socially unequal distribution of expectations becomes the consequence of what is presumed to be a psychological issue' (p. 347); thus as the root cause is seen as fixed, the expectations are also fixed. To elaborate, if we think of ability as a fixed quantity, then it is not a very big leap to argue that there is no point in teaching some children, or allowing some to access other opportunities. Historically this has been the case for minoritised and working-class children, where ability has been used to justify limits to what schools they attend (through the 11+), the exams they sit (Gillborn 2006b), and as we saw earlier, the groups they sit in. As Gillborn and Youdell argue in relation to secondary schools, 'Ability offers a supposedly fair means for condemning some children to second class educations'; it 'acts to legitimate the systematic failing of Black and working-class young people' (Gillborn and Youdell 2001, p. 95). In their research, ability was the underlying structure which maintained and reinforced school practices such as educational triage, which reproduced disparities in attainment. Similarly, I found in my research with Reception pupils (age 4–5) in the late 2000s that the idea of ability offered a clear structuring frame to discussions about pupils' attainment and served to legitimise differential expectations (Bradbury 2013b). Teachers described four- and five-year-old pupils as 'with it', 'clever', 'smart, 'sparky' and 'bright'; and one teacher described a child as 'brighter, or whatever word we should use', suggesting a cynicism about those who might object to such labels. These terms were associated with particular positive learner identities, which were only intelligible in relation to some groups of pupils; in turn these identities as 'high, low or middle' ability pupils were reflected in teacher assessments. Thus children began their school lives with different starting points and expectations, which were, I argued, affected by their racialised and classed identities.

In the Grouping Project, as we have already seen in the previous chapter, there were links made between ability and children's backgrounds: phrases such as 'family input', 'parental support' as indicators of ability refer to classed and raced assumptions about which children's parents are doing the 'right' kind of parenting. Some of this is meant sympathetically, I think, to indicate that children may not be inherently different but simply have different exposure to vocabulary, for instance. But overall there remains a clear link, in some teachers' minds at least, between being 'high ability' and middle class. In a similar vein, this school leader explained how putting children in ability groups in nursery (age 3–4) was necessary because of differences in children's backgrounds:

> 'So last year I taught Nursery and we grouped the children in Nursery as well but it's done in a way that they don't realise they're being grouped or anything. They're not being labelled in any way at all but it's done because, especially in early years, children come to the early years with a lot of different experiences from outside of school ... 60% of the children who are Pupil Premium didn't make their Good Level of Development, so they didn't reach where they should be.' (School Leader, Whiteread Primary)

Here we see how this view that children are affected by their backgrounds – which is why they require teaching in different groups from the age of three – can very quickly switch into a comment about whole groups of children (Pupil Premium children) who come from poorer backgrounds having lower attainment. Although this teacher says 'They're not being labelled in any way' by being put in a lower-ability group, children are labelled as not attaining the GLD benchmark.

The participants also raised concerns about children who spoke English as an additional language (EAL), and their placement in lower-ability groups: "I also want to just talk about children with English as an additional language and the impact that grouping has on them because quite often, especially when they first arrive, they are automatically placed in lower ability" (Focus Group 2 participant). Similarly, a respondent to the survey commented, "The problem with grouping comes with low ability as this tends to group SEN, EAL and behaviour problems all in the same group." Children with EAL, who are more likely to come from minoritised groups, are disproportionately labelled as 'low ability'.

Research more widely 'reinforces the view that ability grouping frequently leads to inequity and deepening disadvantage' (Hamilton and O'Hara 2011, p. 714). The formality of grouping leads to the labelling of some children as 'low ability', with some groups of pupils over-represented in that category. Children from disadvantaged backgrounds and from some ethnic groups are more likely to be in lower sets or groups in both primary and secondary schools (Muijs and Dunne 2010; Dunne et al 2011; Archer et al 2018; Francis et al 2019). For Archer et al, the system of setting by ability

> can be interpreted as a technology of social reproduction, which reflects the interests of the privileged and is designed to maintain social class and racialized inequalities and unequal relations. The legitimacy of setting is maintained through misrecognition, in which students come to understand themselves and others as 'deserving' their set allocation on the basis that the judgements used to assign them are simply reflective of their 'natural' abilities and that segregation is needed in order to protect (to legitimate and not contaminate) the ('better') experiences and attainment of those with higher 'ability' from the 'distracting' presence of Others (those of 'undesirable' ability, dispositions and behaviour). (2018, p. 136)

Thus ability, and its manifestation in grouping, is a form of symbolic violence, they argue, that reinforces and maintains inequalities. McGillicuddy and Devine, in reference to primary schools in Ireland, similarly argue that grouping practices are a 'symbolically violent process that negatively impacts the psychosocial positioning of children'

(2020, p. 553). They found that the more 'pro-ability' grouping teachers in their survey were working in 'the most marginalised schools' (2020, p. 559), and that in their case study schools, children from the white majority were more likely to be in higher groups while African and Traveller children were in lower groups.

These findings reflect a far broader body of work, which has continued to make links between the operation of ability and the permanence of disparities in education related to race and class internationally. For some, the two are irrevocably intertwined: 'race does not exist outside of ability and ability does not exist outside of race' (Annamma et al 2013, p. 6). Similarly, Leonardo and Broderick have argued that, in the context of the US, the two concepts of race and intelligence have been co-constitutive (2011, p. 2216). Globally, the history of producing 'race' as an idea (Omi and Winant 2004) has been a project of systematically labelling some groups as deficient in fixed and inherited ways. The history of working-class (and indeed girls') access to education has similarly included debates on capacity to learn (Reay 2006) (as well, of course, on the need to create a docile class).

Ability is an idea which serves a clear purpose in justifying and maintaining inequalities, although the language may have changed over time. Within the neoliberal meritocratic state, the notion of fixed ability is clouded in the terminology of merit as something solid, despite the fact that merit is a social construct:

> merit is not an inherent personal quality but a set of social produced capabilities underpinned by capitals of different sorts, which ensures that social groups with wealth and heritage, and relevant cultural knowledge and social relations can respond to educational opportunities to assert or reproduce social and economic advantage. (Jin and Ball 2020, p. 65)

Thus when politicians talk about ensuring opportunities or letting everyone go 'as far as their talents take them', this is based on a misrecognition of merit as socially produced, linked to social and economic circumstances.

## The new eugenics?

This section considers the latest developments in relation to race, class and ability, and the dangers posed by a 'new eugenics'. As discussed, the notions of intelligence and ability have always been inflected with raced and classed associations (Chitty 2007; Ball 2013; Gillborn 2016). While the UK context is different, the entanglement of hierarchical notions of intelligence with raced and classed discourses is also long-standing and, as examined earlier, operationalised in everyday school contexts. Nonetheless, there have been many concerns raised in recent years about a resurgence or revival of biological determinism, often based on new findings relating to genetics. I consider here how these long-standing links between hierarchies of intelligence and raced and classed groups are being reinvigorated through current educational and policy discourses, before I go on to discuss the specific cases of neuroscience and datafication in Chapters 4 and 5. There is some overlap between the cases of neuroscience and epigenetics, as discussed in the developing field of biosocial studies in education (Youdell and Lindley 2018), but here I consider the broader relations of genetic developments to inequalities specifically, and how these relate to the neoliberal context of education.

Since the beginning of the neoliberal policy era in England, ability 'has come to be understood (by policymakers and practitioners alike) as a proxy for common-sense notions of "intelligence"' (Gillborn and Youdell 2001, p. 65). Facilitated by the accountability system of high-stakes tests, teachers engaged in the 1990s and 2000s with a new 'IQism' based on fixed intelligence, which provided a foundation for strategies of 'rationing' education with unequal outcomes: 'ability is constituted in ways which provide for the systematic disadvantaging of particular socially defined groups, especially children of working class and Black/African-Caribbean heritage' (Gillborn and Youdell 2001, p. 65). More recently, Gillborn (2010, 2016, 2018) has argued that we can see a revival of the 'crudest and most regressive notion of intelligence/ ability' (Gillborn 2010), which is in part related to a resurgence in scientific racism. The influence of the case of the controversial book *The Bell Curve: Intelligence and Class Structure in American Life* by Richard Herrnstein and Charles Murray in 1994, the resulting public debate and the defence of the book by a number of other scientists, lingers on in conversations about race, class and IQ. Despite the general consternation at the claim of racial difference in IQ and the discrediting of the findings in subsequent texts, the book marks the beginning of an atmosphere which pitted 'science' (or more specifically one specific group of scientists) against social progressives, who were accused of rejecting scientific findings due to their lack of social acceptability. This same desire to 'tell the unacceptable truth' was evident in the book *A Troublesome Inheritance: Genes, Race and Human History* by the ex-*New York Times* journalist Nicholas Wade (2014), which was widely rejected by scientists as an inaccurate representation of their findings. Wade claimed in the book that genetics and culture combined account for differences in economic success by different racial groups. His work was defended by Charles Murray in the *Wall Street Journal*, where he claimed that reactions to the book were further 'proof of this era's intellectual corruption' and evidence of their reluctance to 'explore the way the world really works' (Murray 2014). We see in these defences the echoes of the position of many on the right in the US and Europe who denounce 'political correctness' and the 'snowflake generation' who cannot cope with arguments that do not fit their world view (Haslam-Ormerod 2019). Those who reject unacceptable findings are dismissed as refusing to engage in reality.

Gillborn argues that this atmosphere has altered the conversation in recent years, in response the public revulsion at explicit connections between genes, differential intelligence and race, as exemplified in the case of the public outcry about comments on the topic by the Nobel Prize-winning scientist James Watson in 2007 (Gillborn 2016). Watson was publicly vilified, demonstrating the broader distaste and unacceptability of comments which use scientific findings to claim deterministic differences between 'races'. This has not stopped some public figures making claims about genes and intelligence, as we have seen in the quotes from Boris Johnson already mentioned. Instead, the tone of the debate has shifted to what Gillborn characterises as a 'softly softly' approach, here quoting a prominent hereditarian geneticist Robert Plomin's own description of his strategy to avoid controversy (Gillborn 2016). In this time of *inexplicitness*, specific mentions of race are rare; instead 'race hovers in the background' (Gillborn 2016, p. 371). Thus 'the new geneism adopts a colourblind meritocratic and celebratory tone whereby race is rarely mentioned at all and the supposed 'advances' are hailed as good news for everyone' (2016, p. 366). As Jackson puts it, 'This "science is apolitical" merry-go-round needs to stop' (2014, p. 205). Within this, those who critique the racist connotations of claims are dismissed as prejudiced, failing to understand the science, or as irrational (Gillborn 2016, p. 369). The reaction to comments such as Watson's does not mean, however, that these ideas have no power: the response reveals

> general revulsion – at least in terms of overt statements – generated by crude attempts to assert a link between race

and intelligence. And yet the tragic irony of UK education is that policy-makers act as if they fundamentally accept the same simple view of intelligence (as a relatively fixed and measurable quality that differs between individuals). Crucially, however, the word 'intelligence' is rarely used; policy-makers and teachers substitute different terms, such as 'ability' or 'potential'. (Gillborn 2010, p. 243)

It also does not mean that these beliefs have gone away: 'hereditarians have not changed their mind about race and intelligence – they just don't broadcast it any more' (Gillborn 2016, p. 382). As various policy documents from the 2000s reveal, the use of 'potential' has grown (Gillborn 2010); this I would argue continued in the 2010s, where the claim that the school system must allow everyone to 'go as far as their talents can take them' remained prominent. These are biopolitical discourses which work to exclude sectors of the population from educatable status: 'New eugenic discourses ... establish some people as pollutants or detractors. Even where such classifications are thought to be for the benefit of the recipient, they cannot be disarticulated from populational governance strategies' (Baker 2002).

For Gillborn, this use of 'potential' represents a further example of how ideas of fixed intelligence or limits to learning persist, and therefore the inequities which result remain unchallenged. As a result, unless we engage in critique, 'we may find that scientific racism has reshaped our education systems without even mentioning race' (Gillborn 2016, p. 382).

## The epigenetic challenge to determinism and race

The curious paradox within these uses of genetic research to discuss racial differences is that there are many who argue that findings about genes, and particularly the interaction between environment and genes, produce a serious challenge to the deterministic understandings of genetics and race and class which dominated the twentieth century. Certainly, there is potential for these new developments to disrupt the simplistic notions of genetic determinism, particularly through recognition of plasticity and challenges to heredity. Meloni (2017) raises the question of what the postgenomic era means for our understandings of race as an idea. In particular, he asks what scientific discussions of how the environments can affect genes, where these altered genes are then passed on to subsequent generations, mean for notions of heredity. Using examples of studies on racial health differences, such as lower average birth weights for African-American babies which are related to the physical outcomes of slavery, Meloni considers how these new developments may interact with older notions of group difference. He argues that 'if sociologists want to investigate race in a post-genomic world then they should pay more attention to this novel plastic and biosocial view of race' (2017, p. 389).[7]

However, the hopeful claims that epigenetics may result in more nuanced debates about intelligence and social characteristics may be overly optimistic. Youdell warns,

> there has been a lot of concern over the potential uses of epigenetics – the finer and finer grained management of populations; the further entrenchment of individualisation and responsibilisation ... the rearticulation of dividing practices that racialise and are marked by gender, sexuality, social class; the validation or even promotion, or the optimisation of the person. (Youdell 2016, p. 800)

In relation to class, Dorling and Tomlinson comment, 'while epigenetic research is engaging with what the environment does to gene expressions and the functioning of the body at the molecular level, work on generalised intelligence is heading in the opposite direction', remaining focused on the idea that 'social class and intelligence will ultimately be shown to be genetic' (2016, p. 789).

Meloni warns that the move towards 'soft' inheritance may not provide the disruption to old associations that is hoped for, arguing 'there are no reasons to believe that an epigenetic view will extinguish race, or that soft-inheritance claims will produce a less exclusionary discourse than genetics (hard heredity)' (2017, p. 389). Nonetheless, the idea that past ideas have simply been 'resuscitated', described as 'a continuous view of postgenomics as a *mere prolongation of the old genomics business*' (2017, p. 390, emphasis in original), fails to recognise the pluralistic way in which race may be framed in the postgenomic era. For Meloni, then, the risk is that in failing to appreciate the variety of ways in which race may be biologically framed in this new era, we also ignore 'a more pernicious potential for racialist discourses than genomics had in a recent past' (2017, p. 391). Looking at this argument through the lens of CRT, we can see how the postgenomic era may be seen as producing a *different, but still damaging* view of race and genetics and the environment. The idea, for example, that different birth weights may be a result of a complex interaction of genes and environment over generations is no less deterministic in its outcomes than pure genetics. It does not take too many steps, then, to see how epigenetic arguments could be used to reproduce, in more complex ways, discourses of inevitable disparities in attainment. After all, racism is 'relentless, yet fluid, and quick to morph depending on current circumstances' (Gillborn 2018, p. 66). Similarly, Youdell, in her far more positive discussions of the contributions of biology to the study of education, recognises the very real dangers that new science will be used to reproduce old inequalities (Youdell 2017). There is a danger of a new determinism based on epigenetics; this new science 'can conceivably produce a new twist on prior historical debates about which populations, often racialised, to fund educationally, and which populations not to fund' (Gulson and Webb 2018, p. 282).

## Inequality and education in the era of COVID-19

The fluidity of racism, and the continued issue of recognising different experiences without homogenising entire communities, were clear in discussion of the differential impact of the COVID-19 pandemic on minoritised groups during the first phase of the pandemic in 2020. Within this important debate, frequent references to the relative disadvantage of some ethnic groups and mention of cultural practices such as inter-generational households demonstrated a continued project of othering and homogenisation. Then, towards the end of the spring 2020 lockdown period in the UK, the extent and spread of Black Lives Matter protests around the world, following the murder of George Floyd by US police officers, again brought issues of racial equity to the fore in public debate. When a statue of a slave trader was pulled down by protestors in Bristol and dumped in a canal, this triggered a broader discussion of Britain's racist imperial legacy and its contemporary manifestations (Weale et al 2020). The reaction of some to these debates – from the racist thuggery of riots in Westminster to the right-wing commentators decrying the idea of removing statues, and the prime minister's comment that attacking statues is 'lying about our history' (Giordano 2020) – revealed the extent to which perceptions of racial difference remain a problematic feature of the social landscape in Britain. Indeed, in the same comments, Boris Johnson looked to education to defend the government's record on racial equality, arguing:

> I think this is a country that has made huge progress in tackling racism. We should look sometimes at the positive stuff – we've got more young black and minority ethnic

kids going to university than ever before, more black kids doing the tougher subjects at school, doing better than ever before in school. We don't hear enough of this positive stuff. (Boris Johnson, June 2020 cited in Giordano 2020)

This explanation, that the 'positive stuff' of improved university attendance and 'black kids doing tougher subjects', was not prominent enough, reveals the distance between the vision of equality espoused by protestors and the prime minister's notion of progress. Johnson appears to suggest that minoritised communities should be grateful for these steps, for not getting an 'easy ride' at school, instead of protesting against structural inequality: his examples are evidence of how education is co-opted as part of the meritocratic social mobility discourse which emphasises 'opportunity' over injustice. While there may be some positive figures to point to in education, as we have seen in this chapter, educational inequalities – by race and class – remain a powerful features of the education system.

A major concern during the spring 2020 lockdown period of the COVID-19 pandemic in the UK was the differences in experiences of children learning at home, and how this would exacerbate gaps in attainment between children from disadvantaged backgrounds and their wealthier peers. The terms of this discussion showed how embedded associations between 'disadvantaged' children and low educational achievement have become. A well-publicised report from the Education Endowment Foundation argued that a decade of progress in reducing the attainment gap could be reversed by the pandemic (EEF 2020) because having schools closed to most children for months would disproportionately affect 'poorer' children. The Institute for Fiscal Studies (IFS) reported that 'Children from better-off families are spending 30% more time on home learning than are those from poorer families' (IFS 2020); this difference would amount to 15 schools days' difference over the whole lockdown period. They concluded:

> *School closures are almost certain to increase educational inequalities.* Pupils from better-off families are spending longer on home learning; they have access to more individualised resources such as private tutoring or chats with teachers; they have a better home set-up for distance learning; and their parents report feeling more able to support them. Policymakers should already be thinking about how to address the gaps in education that the crisis is widening. (IFS 2020, emphasis in original)

Furthermore, much of the discussion about the need to reopen schools after lockdown and the need for a 'catch up' programme centred on the assumption that children from poorer families would have spent less time on home learning. The Education Endowment Foundation (EEF), for instance, proposed a national programme of tutoring.

There is no doubt that material differences made a difference to children's experiences of lockdown (Moss et al 2020). The concern for children from disadvantaged families focused in part upon food, and the provision of FSM via deliveries or vouchers (Burns 2020), and in part on the 'digital divide' in terms of access to online home learning (Casciani 2020; Coughlan 2020). This latter concern was complicated by the failure of the government to provide promised free laptops to pupils (Carr 2020). The IFS reported that 'More than half (58%) of primary school students from the least well-off families do not have access to their own study space' (IFS 2020); while a report based on the UK Household Longitudinal Study found that a fifth of students on FSM had no access to a computer at home, compared to 7 per cent of other children (Green 2020).

However, as well as these concerns about material disadvantages, there were also some familiar tropes relating to the inability or reluctance of some parents to teach their children at home, which, I would argue, reproduce a deficit discourse of particular families as lazy, unwilling to help themselves, and having the wrong priorities.[8] During the first lockdown period of March to June 2020, a popular 'discourse of derision' emerged which 'suggests that children need saving from their parents, who can't, or won't, work within the school's value system' (Byrd 2020, p. 348). This is often aimed at working-class parents, who fail to ascribe to the middle-class expectations of parenting (Vincent and Ball 2007). For instance, a government minister was accused of 'demonising' families on FSM by suggesting they were spending the vouchers provided to replace school meals on alcohol (Roberts 2020). Disadvantaged children were described by the Secretary of State for Education as in greater need of schools to avoid 'miss[ing] out on the opportunities and chances in life that we want all children to benefit from' (Williamson 2020). The idea that poorer children would require more 'catching up' became well established, adding a further layer of deficit thinking in relation to this group.

This is a complex issue, and one which will continue to develop as disruption due to COVID-19 continues. Research in which I participated in May–October 2020 found that schools had had very different experiences of the pandemic (Moss et al 2020) but that teachers had gained a better knowledge of their communities. We found that there was increased awareness of the difficulties faced by families in terms of material poverty, and an overwhelming commitment to children's welfare (and particularly to feeding children) over teaching (Bradbury and Duncan 2020). One key outcome of the pandemic may be a wider awareness of the inequalities of society – as shown by the popular campaign by footballer Marcus Rashford to provide free meals in school holidays. This awareness might lead to more critical thinking about the idea of meritocracy as we recognise how material deprivation might have an impact in ways which may appear to reflect children's innate ability. I return to this topic in the final chapter.

## Conclusion

This chapter has set out some of the ways in which the idea of ability and intelligence have worked and are working to produce and maintain educational inequalities. By focusing on education outcomes, I aimed to show that – however we might question their production and accuracy, as I have done extensively – the school system in England results in disparities in qualifications by ethnic group and social class which are extensive and persistent. The system of neoliberal meritocracy operates as an 'ideological myth to obscure inequalities, including the role this discourse itself plays in actually curtailing social mobility' (Littler 2017, p. 50). As Reay argues, 'A meritocratic system is a competition in which there are clear winners and losers, but in which the resulting inequalities are justified on the basis that participants have an equal opportunity to prove themselves' (Reay 2020b, p. 405). These disparities have real significance for the young people involved, not least in how they see themselves as students and their access to further levels of study and employment. Debates over issues of race and class in education have been dominated in the last decade by concern over institutional racism, the significance of 'model minorities', and a refocusing on the white working class as the 'victims'. These debates have shifted, however, in the era of COVID-19, with a renewed focus on racial inequality due to Black Lives Matter campaigns and repeated connections made between poorer children and 'learning loss' under lockdown. The chapter described how notions of ability and intelligence have historically been related to inequalities, and continue to be so in contemporary schools, despite their dismissal by scientists. As Morning (2014) comments about the return of biological race to the field of social sciences, 'And you thought we had moved beyond all that'.

The penultimate section of the chapter focused on the potential, in both negative and positive terms, for new developments in the postgenomic era to disrupt or reignite discourses of intelligence as determined and fixed and varying among different social groups. In particular, I want to emphasise the warning that 'racial geneism – the belief that genes shape the nature of ethnic group achievements and inequities – has returned with a vengeance but in a new and more dangerous form' (Gillborn 2016, p. 366). The context of a worldwide pandemic in which discussions of the impact of school closures on 'disadvantaged' children were so prominent only makes this comment more relevant: a time of instability allows for the return of dangerous thinking as much as it offers hope for radical change.

In the following chapters I argue that, through their interaction with the concept of ability, the adoption of neuroscience and the increased use of data also have the potential to reproduce and exacerbate the inequities by race and class examined here.

# 4

# The influence of neuroscience

## Introduction

This chapter focuses on the first of the two education trends, the growing influence of neuroscience. I begin by examining the influence of neuroscience in the broadest sense, before considering the 'neuroturn' (De Vos 2017) in education specifically. This is followed by a discussion of the doubts and dangers of using neuroscientific findings in simplistic ways in real life contexts, including in classrooms. I then turn to the interaction between neuroscience and the concept of ability, while a final section explores the inequalities that can be reproduced through a focus on the brain as a symbol for different abilities.

Throughout this chapter, I do not make any claims as to the quality of neuroscientific research, as I am not qualified to do so; rather my focus is on the ways in which this 'new knowledge' (McGimpsey et al 2017) filters into wider discourses about children and the effects this has on inequalities. The brain has always been ideologically constructed in importance, such as in historic efforts to measure the size of skulls and relate them to class, gender and race (Richardson 2017); what I argue here is that the growth of neuroscience and its powerful influence on policy in recent years represent a *reworking of discourses of determinism related to background*, to which we must focus our attention, particularly given the repeated connections made in popular debate between background and the impact of the COVID-19 pandemic on learning. This crisis has facilitated further focus on children's brains.

## The 'new neuros'

In this section I set out some key points relating to the growth in influence of neuroscience, and the resultant criticisms. Here I draw on a range of literature from both scientists and social scientists, and particularly that from the emerging field of critical neuroscience. This area of study focuses on the problematic ways in which ideas purportedly from the new brain sciences are translated into everyday practice and policy. In reviewing this field, I want to emphasise two salient points:

- First, that everything 'neuro' is regarded as fashionable, hyped and as cutting-edge science, despite the complexity of the field and its relative youth (Pykett 2012). Competing claims and ambiguities are glossed over in the attempt to present the 'insights' from this 'new knowledge' as revolutionary in our understanding of human nature and potential (McGimpsey et al 2017).
- Second, a key theme in the discussion of how neuroscience is operationalised is that translation into real life situations (such as classrooms) of these 'insights' is always problematic. There is danger of simplification of complex findings and the misapplication of 'new' ideas to re-inscribe older notions of hierarchy and deficit.

The influence of neuroscience and its application to contexts outside the laboratory have grown significantly since the 1990s were declared the 'decade of the brain'. Technological advances in our ability to scan and capture the brain as it works have allowed for neuroscientific studies to proliferate and impact on the public consciousness as never before. The fast-moving experimental methodology of neuroscience, using ever-more detailed ways of scanning or capturing the brain's activity (Kitchen 2017, p. 7) make it an exciting and dynamic field. Momentum is growing in the use of the resulting discourses relating to these brain sciences (Billington 2017), and now at the end of the second decade of the new 'century of the brain', there is no sign of the hype surrounding the 'insights' from neuroscience abating. As Pykett comments, the 'trend towards neuroscientific explanation appears unstoppable in its popularity and reach, with the "neuro" prefix finding more and more endings and applications' (2012, p. 864); these are the 'new neuros'.

Part of this allure arises from the sheer novelty of the field; neuroscience is seen as a young area of study with great potential to change people's lives. Although it grew out of a long trajectory of brain sciences and the study of the nervous system, an 'epistemological shift' has occurred since the 1960s whereby breakthroughs in understanding the brain were constructed as crucial (Abi-Rached and Rose 2010). There are clear links and overlaps with areas of biology, physiology and psychology (Kitchen 2017). Neuroscience can be 'broadly defined' thus:

> [Neuroscience] investigates the processes by which the brain learns and remembers, from the molecular and cellular levels right through to brain systems (e.g., the system of neural areas and pathways underpinning our ability to speak and

comprehend language). This focus on learning and memory
can be at a variety of levels. (Goswami 2004, p. 1)

This connection to learning makes applying new findings to education
and other social settings inevitably attractive, not least for policy makers
keen to justify their latest approach; the terms 'hope' and 'excitement'
frequently feature in discussions of their potential. Neuroscience and
education seem 'natural partners' (Kitchen 2017, p. 5). But while
the field of brain sciences is relatively new and inevitably complex
and contested, these complexities are frequently lost when findings
are translated into recommendations for professionals, who are
seduced by the scientific allure of the neuroscience term. A general
lack of neuroscience literacy means this field is 'especially vulnerable
to misunderstanding and misappropriation' (Busso and Pollack
2015, p. 168).

Discussions about the dominance of 'neuro' ideas abound; as De
Vos and Pluth argue, 'the prefix neuro- has won its final battle … It
has conquered critique itself' (2015, p. 22). This ubiquity masks the
complexity of real lives and individuals; De Vos and Pluth criticise the
attempts drawn from neuroscience to 'convince everybody that we are
our brain, that we should be our brain, that we have to become our
brain' (2015, p. 38). There is danger in the simplified conclusion that
our brains are enough to understand us and what we should do with
our lives; that a hegemonic neural subjectivity develops, described as
the 'neurochemical self' (Rose 2001). This theme of the irreducibility
of the individual to their brain is common in the field of critical
neuroscience, which seeks to resist this reductionism and the related
determinism and essentialism.

The influence of neuroscience can also be related to the developments
in other scientific fields such as genetics, which have similarly been
lauded as revolutionary in our understanding of human lives and
potential. The sequencing of the human genome and the development
of genetic testing have reignited discussions of deterministic hereditable
characteristics and the influence of the environment. Epigenetics,
which focuses on the relationship between genes and environment,
suggests 'Environmental inputs … impact the brain initially patterned
by the genome', producing 'a new story about the brain in/and society'
(Pickersgill 2018, p. 103). Pickersgill characterises these combinations
of genetics and neuroscience as the 'imagined biological', which
'might often emphasise the brain, but shifts between other icons of
somatic concern also feature prominently' (Pickersgill 2018, p. 101).

Although my focus here is on neuroscience, the wider impact of circulating discourses relating to genetically determined characteristics and dispositions provides an important part of the context. Indeed, this broader concern with 'new biological rationalities' in education has recently been the subject of special issue and various papers in education (Youdell 2017; Gulson and Baker 2018; Youdell et al 2018). I return to the topic of biosocial education in later sections.

## The neuroturn in education

Education (as well as social policy) is an area which has been particularly susceptible to the proliferation of neuroscience, for both political and commercial reasons. This influence has been referred to as the 'neuro turn' in education (De Vos 2017). Pykett comments: 'Neuroscientific insights are now regarded as crucial to the development of learning theories and educational research, with major research programmes being funded both in the UK and USA in the emerging field of neuroducation' (Pykett 2012, p. 846). Within academia, this influence can be seen in the establishment of journals such as *Mind, Brain and Education* in 2007 and special interest groups within national education research associations (Baker 2015). Looking at practices in schools and parenting advice, De Vos argues, could lead us to speak, more dramatically, of 'a neuro-tsunami, hailing everybody, both pupil and parent, into the neuro-discourse' (2016, p. 130).

Insights from brain science are regarded as significant in our understanding of how children learn, how best to teach and how to provide stimulating learning environments. The most popular signs of this in schools are the much-criticised practices labelled 'brain gym' which were popular in the 2000s (Geake 2005, cited in Purdy and Morrison 2009). These were exercises such as pressing your 'brain buttons', which were seen as preparing children for learning, based on new information science provided about brain functioning (and I confess to using these as a new teacher in the mid-2000s, having learnt them on my Postgraduate Certificate in Education course). Also popular for a time was the practice of labelling children as visual, auditory or kinaesthetic (VAK) learners (with children wearing VAK badges in some schools) and adapting lessons so that all different types of learner were covered. Again, I remember having to fill in the VAK box on every lesson plan to demonstrate how I covered these three learning styles. While these fads catered for schools' 'hunger … for more information about the brain' (Goswami 2006, p. 2), tapping into a market based on the enthusiasm for new insights, they were often based on spurious or oversimplified versions of findings from neuroscience. As Goswami comments, 'Some popular beliefs about what brain science can actually deliver to education are quite unrealistic. Although current brain science technologies offer exciting opportunities to educationists, they complement rather than replace traditional methods of educational enquiry' (2004, p. 2).

As such, neuroscience is an example of what I (with colleagues) have called elsewhere, a 'new knowledge' in policy: that is, 'articulated sets of concepts and "facts", typically originating (or seemingly originating) in named fields of academic work ... often presented as entirely new, very credible, homogenous in their conclusions, and disruptive of existing ideas within policy-making' (McGimpsey et al 2017, p. 909). These new knowledges provide justificatory narratives for policy makers. For example, Purdy and Morrison (2009) argue that the neuroscientific justification for the Revised Curriculum in Northern Ireland from 2007 is based on a flawed understanding of findings about 'connectedness'. The resulting discrediting of teaching in discrete subjects has no basis in neuroscience, but this justification 'adds a veneer of scientific respectability' (2009, p. 107).

More recently, there has been some empirical research on the processes through which neuroscience influences policy and practice. Broer and Pickersgill's interviews with policy makers and professionals in Scotland demonstrate how 'neuroscientific knowledge is employed to imbue policies and practices with epistemic authority' (2015a, p. 53) Findings from brain science are used to lend credibility to ideas when applying for funding, and confirm existing priorities, providing 'firmer epistemological footing for "common-sense" ideas about care and love' (2015a, p. 54). Respondents were wary, however, and reflexive about their use of neuroscience, leading the authors to conclude theirs was a strategy of 'pragmatic reductionism', where neuroscience was used for particular ends. Similarly, in Edwards et al's (2015) research on early intervention and use of neuroscientific explanations, practitioners were enthusiastic about how neuroscience could be used to prove their existing ideas around attachment theory; the Family Nurse Partnership programme they studied delivered a sheet entitled 'How to build your baby's brain' to new mothers. Another participant working in a children's centre had a photograph of a brain scan which he saw as motivating him to improve children's lives, 'rather than just give in to what society might think is okay' (2015, p. 180). From both these studies, we see how neuroscience is used to justify decisions in early years in particular. This sector has been most influenced by the brain sciences, largely due to the 'myth of the first three years' (Bruer 1999).

This myth has implications, as I discuss in a later section, for education more widely.

## The first three years

There is one finding from neuroscience which has affected policy and discourses around brains and potential more than any other: the idea that the first three years of a child's life are crucial for their development, a 'critical period'. This, and the related 'neuromyth' (to use the Organisation for Economic Co-operation and Development's (OECD) phrase) that there are critical periods when certain matters must be taught and learnt (or it is too late) (OECD 2008) are frequently cited in justifications for policy such as early intervention. This myth draws on three neuroscientific insights, summarised by White and Wastell (2017) from Bruer's analysis, as first, 'biological exuberance' of brain connectivity in the first three years, followed by a plateau; secondly, the notion of a 'critical period' of particular importance; and thirdly, that richer environments aid brain development and increase 'brain power' (2017, pp. 41–2). However, 'There is no direct neuroscientific evidence, for either animals or humans, linking adult synaptic density to greater learning capacity' (OECD 2008, p. 110), thus reducing the implications for how we think about learning. Although some of these findings are based on studies of rats reared in different environments, these ideas have been distilled and translated into an overall conclusion that a child's brain is largely fixed by the age of three. As Bruer highlighted in the late 1990s, this is a huge simplification of the idea that there are more optimal periods for learning particular things, which has been allowed to proliferate well beyond the brain sciences (Bruer 1999). Many neuroscientists have battled to redress this reductionism, instead emphasising that 'optimal periods for certain types of learning clearly exist in development, but they are sensitive periods rather than critical ones' (Goswami 2004, p. 11). Yet, the dominance of the first three years myth continued into the 2010s: it is repeatedly used in policy documents, and in early 2019 a new *All Party Parliamentary Group for Conception to Age 2 – the First 1001 Days* was formed, driven by the need to focus on the first three years (UK Parliament 2020).

During the Coalition Government era, a much-discussed series of reports on Early Intervention produced by the Centre for Social Justice (CSJ) think tank demonstrated this explicit recourse to new ideas from neuroscience to justify social policy; for example: 'The quality of a child's primary caregiver's support and nurture profoundly influences a child's very early formative years. Their first three years are critical in terms of the brain's social, emotional and physical development' (2011b, pp. 14–15).

We see here how powerful the first three years discourse can be in framing the debate over early childhood education and care. As I have argued (with colleagues) elsewhere, in these reports neuroscience facilitates three processes: 'the constitution of the family and the family environment as a key site of policy intervention; the constitution of the neurologically damaged child as a policy problem; and the justification of spending on early intervention as a preventative measure based on principles of economic efficiency' (McGimpsey et al 2017, p. 912). This 'new emphasis on the neurologically "damaged child"' (Lowe et al 2015b, p. 17) reaches far back into discussion of the impact of maternal mental health and behaviour on the developing foetus, despite the lack of current evidence that babies' brains are determined by mothers' levels of stress, for example. I return to the constitution of the neurologically damaged child as a policy problem in later sections but wish to emphasise here the significance of neuroscience within early intervention policy as a justificatory narrative (see also Edwards et al 2015; Gillies et al 2017). It is clear that this idea 'sparks the imaginations and hopes of policymakers' (Broer and Pickersgill 2015a, p. 47), though there are potentially significant implication for the child as a subject of policy. Before I turn to the connections to inequalities, I first consider the overall doubts about the use of neuroscience and the reasons for its popularity.

## The doubts and dangers

Given the complexity of the field of brain sciences and the continued debates within it, it is perhaps not surprising that there has been some criticism of how neuroscientific findings have been presented in the press and translated into policy and practice. Nonetheless, the scale of criticism and doubt that surround findings from neuroscience and the attention given to both the original science and its movement into the wider world suggest that these questions go beyond the usual level of academic debate. Neuroscience is a field at risk of 'brain overclaim syndrome' (Rose 2010, p. 81), particularly where findings from animals are transferred to humans. Scientific findings are 'mostly used in reductionist and overtly deterministic fashion in social policy, health and education sciences', and never used 'in purified form in societal and political processes' (Millei and Joronen 2016, p. 390). Significantly, there are neuroscientists who proclaim that 'At present, there are no findings from neuroscience that have implications for classroom practice' (Coltheart, cited in Vandenbroeck and Olsson 2017, p. 84); thus the entire project of translating this scientific field is seen by some as flawed. Others see the problem as 'translation gone awry': 'the translation is the problem – highly specialised and highly limited findings *cannot* be extrapolated to make general prescriptions about social policy' (Penn 2017, p. 58 in reference to Rutter and Solantaus, 2014, emphasis in original). Van Ommen summarises: 'the danger of neuroscience is that as it colonies social notions it almost inevitably impoverishes them, reduces their play of meaning, their polysemity, and empties them out, rendering them manageable, controllable, and inflict-able; that is, as a measurable quantity against which the other can be found lacking' (van Ommen 2013, p. 12).

Examples abound of the over-simplification of findings and their shift into real-life situations. The OECD report details several 'neuromyths' such as: that you can learn while you sleep; that we only use 10 per cent of our brains; that there are left brains and right brains; that there are gender differences in brains; that a child can only learn one language at a time; and that memory can be improved. Many of these have commercial implications or have been used to justify interventions in policy and practice. As discussed, one of the most notable and relevant to the discussion that follows is the 'myth of the first three years' (Bruer 1999), the idea that the first three years of a child's life are vital in determining their brain development. These ideas have been used in problematic ways, for example, in influencing courts' decisions to remove children from their parents on the basis that there is a critical period where intervention is vital. Thus 'Professionals are increasingly incorporating neuroscience into their everyday vocabularies of risk' (White and Wastell 2017, p. 46). We also see a similar tendency in criminal justice policy, where the approach of 'screen and intervene' has been taken in relation to individuals judged as 'damaged' (Rose 2010). The lesson from neuroscience is seen as being that some people have 'risky brains', while others do not. The step from this to social policy is clear; the state should intervene to reduce the impact of these risky or damaged brains.

Other examples of translation gone awry include the idea that neuroscience has 'discovered' number sense or numerosity (the quantity of a set of items) in animals and human infants and related it to areas of the brain. This idea was widely reported and began to be understood as the basis for mathematical understanding (and the differences in the population in attainment in maths). The idea of number sense thus influenced how we understand disculculia and relate this condition to a deficiency in one area of the brain. However, as Fias (2017) argues, there are a number of fundamental flaws in this 'discovery' which illustrate how neuroscience is 'not a static domain of knowledge' and 'in neuroscience the objective truth is an illusory myth' (2017, p. 68). As such, the finding ignores the heterogeneity of dyscalculia and renders ineffective the training programmes based upon it. The lesson to learn, Fias emphasises, is that findings from neuroscience should always be used with care and an awareness of the tendency towards simplification.

A significant danger appears to lie in reducing the individual to their brain, and using this to classify and sort people. The 'brain cannot stand in for the person' (Kirmayer and Gold 2012, p. 315, cited in Billington 2017, p. 873), separate from their experiences and conditions. This is not, after all, how we live our lives: as Billington points out, 'Teachers ... spend their lives neither with brains nor with neural properties but *with persons*' (Billington 2017, p. 873, emphasis added). Neuroeducational discourse is based on 'a machinic conception of the brain and a computational account of learning' (Williamson et al 2018, p. 260); metaphors of the brain as like a phone with evolving technology are examples of dangerous reductionism. Some argue that we cannot use anything we know about how a brain functions to understand more complex concepts such as learning or wisdom, or, indeed, the emotional elements of education; those that confuse knowledge about the brain with knowledge about learning are guilty of a 'category mistake' (Davis 2004).

To address these concerns, there have been calls for greater collaboration between neuroscientists and educationists to help bridge the divides and reduce the misappropriation of brain science (Howard-Jones 2011; Billington 2017). There are many differences in approach which stymie productive interdisciplinary work: for example, 'words such as "motivation", "reward", "attention" and even "learning" appear to have different meanings within neuroscience and education' (Howard-Jones 2011). Working together might reduce the 'faulty interpretations, questionable extrapolations, and, more generally, the genesis of false ideas' which have thus far dominated the use of the field (OECD 2008, p. 108). Others are more optimistic about the potential use of neuroscience (Goswami 2006), despite the neuromyths, but argue that 'the educational value of insights from neuroscience rest on their integration with knowledge from more established educational perspectives' (Howard-Jones 2011).

## The view from early childhood education

Critiques of neuroscience in education draw on and have a great deal to learn from scholars in early childhood education (ECE), a sector which has a history of critique of and challenge to scientific discourse, mainly from developmental psychology (Dahlberg and Moss 2005; Yelland 2010; Moss 2015). The examination of how discourses related to 'natural' processes of development and the 'normal' child have been translated from psychology into ECE practice provides an example of how we can unpick the influence of deterministic and damaging discourses based on the pseudo-authenticity of science. Notably, much of the current discourse relating to young children aligns with the longer-standing scientific discourse of development and 'developmentally appropriate practice', which predicts how children change and learn through developmental milestones. This discourse 'has been enlivened by the use of "insights" from neuroscience, which have provided reassurance and credibility to this modernist perspective of children's progress' (McGimpsey et al 2017, p. 912).

Recently, these critiques in ECE have included analyses of the growing importance of neuroscience on the sector. Vandenbroeck describes his work as a history of the present abuses of neurosciences; he draws attention to the ways in which neuroscience discourses obscure the impact on poverty (a topic I return to later) and construct ECE as 'an investment on which we expect an economic return' (2017, p. 1). This latter human capital-inspired conception of ECE, which draws heavily on the neuromyth of the crucial birth to three years, can be seen in 'a neurobiological–economic nexus in which childhood is merely the preamble of adult productivity in a meritocratic society' (2017, p. 13). Investment in early education is justified through the cost-benefit ration of spending money early, in order to ensure children have brains that will not cause problems later. Similarly, based on work in Australian ECE, Millei and Joronen argue that neuroscience has been politicised and has become a dominant framework which provides a new 'hopeful ethos' for human capital theory (Millei and Joronen 2016). These political and economic connections were evident in the now infamous cover of one of the aforementioned Early Intervention reports ('Smart Investment, Massive Savings'), which displayed a pile of gold bars labelled 'teen pregnancy', 'shorter life', 'violent crime' and other social problems next to a single bar labelled 'early intervention', under the heading 'Costs to taxpayer' (Allen 2011b). I return to these themes in the following sections. One of my intentions here is to consider how these critical ideas from ECE can be applied to educational use of neuroscience more broadly.

## Understanding the attraction of neuroscience

So, why is this field so popular and yet so vulnerable to misappropriation? The answer lies perhaps in our desire to understand ourselves and our own brains, and our desire for measurement; as Fias, himself a neuroscientist, argues, there is an 'intuitive conviction that being able to measure something in the brain brings us to a point where our knowledge is objective and indubitable, not needed nor deserving further attention' (Fias 2017, p. 69). Our desire for 'hard science' to find answers is well established and the rhetorical influence of any discussion of the brain, and particularly images of brains, has been found in research (Busso and Pollack 2015, citing Uttal 2011 and McCabe and Castel 2008). As Wastell and White, who have written widely on the misuse of neuroscience, argue, 'it does not really matter what the research papers say, so long as the brain is mentioned' (2017, p. 42). Using neuroscience to improve education 'has a commonsense feel about it' (Howard-Jones 2011), while there are 'general societal tendencies that may cause some ideas to receive more attraction than is justified by the facts' (Fias 2017, p. 77). Thus cases where the science seemingly backs up ideas already in circulation are more likely to gain traction; as a result, the case of differences between male and female brains is particularly popular (OECD 2008). The idea that neuroscience simply repeats long-established tropes around background and brains, innate intelligence and the hierarchical is frequent in critical neuroscience (Abi-Rached and Rose 2010). Many note that there are continuities with existing orthodoxies, such as an 'enduring concordance between biological and economic epistemologies' (Pykett 2012, p. 864). In education, neuroscientific findings resonate with concepts previously seen as drawn from developmental psychology (Billington 2017). These similarities make many findings from neuroscience simply re-inscriptions of existing concepts, such as the idea of fixed ability.

We must also bear in mind the political and commercial motivations for some of bringing neuroscience into the public domain, or as Dumit puts it, 'interrogate the power that so easily speaks in the name of neuroscience' (2015, p. 223). As discussed later in more detail, neuroscience is used in policy documentation as a 'justificatory narrative', lending weight to social policy (McGimpsey et al 2017; Pickersgill 2018). But there are also financial incentives: Pykett notes that at least 88 neuroscience institutes and for-profit organisations had emerged in the US by 2004 (2012, p. 859, citing Ulshofer 2008), while Pickersgill argues that capital 'can be generated through newly and re-configured relationships between life, science and business'

(2018, p. 99). The Harvard Center on the Developing Child provides an example of how neuroscience has been subject to 'sophisticated messaging and artful simplification' in a deliberate attempt to increase its influence on policy (Wastell and White 2012, p. 38). This 'sound bite science', in conjunction with a communications agency, has been highly effective in persuading policy makers of the importance of the field and creating a 'core story' focused on the importance of the early years (2012, p. 40). Examples of commercial applications and the use of neuroscience in advertising educational training and products illustrate further the seductive allure of neuro-discourse (Busso and Pollack 2015).

It is also important to note the power of brain scans as a visual symbol (Abi-Rached and Rose 2010); these are 'reduced to glossy magazine images claiming to reveal the normative infant, adolescent, ADHD or autistic brain or even the brain of a normative abused or neglected infant' (Billington 2017, p. 874). These images combine authority from science with 'appeal to market forces' and 'thirst for technological innovation' (2017, p. 874). McCabe and Castel have demonstrated that research is seen as higher quality when brain images are included (cited in Busso and Pollack 2015, p. 171); they carry great weight in terms of perceptions of scientific veracity. There are good reasons why commercial companies use images of typical and atypical brains to sell their services, and think tanks use them on the covers of reports. These are not neutral, objective, 'scientific' images, however, but through their labelling and juxtaposition with 'normal' brains they become pictorial representations of biological fixity. They suggest 'qualitatively different *brain-types*' (Busso and Pollack 2015, p. 173, emphasis in original) and define who fits into which category and how they should be taught. Thus, like the numerical power of the IQ test before it, the brain scan becomes an ideological tool which reinforces a specific discourse of brains that are normal and abnormal, teachable and in need of alternative 'treatment'. I return to this theme in the second part of this chapter.

There are also broader political motivations to the use of brain sciences, some claim; neuroscience is used 'for political aims that are way beyond the evidence produced' (Vandenbroeck and Olsson 2017, p. 84). The discourses of brain science provide a perfect fit for the neoliberal model of governance, which relies on individualism, entrepreneurship and a meritocratic discourse. Human capital theory, focused on the economic benefits of realising individual potential, goes hand in hand with the idea that we save overall by investing in early education that improves children's brains (Millei and Joronen

2016). Vandenbroeck describes 'a neurobiological nexus in which childhood is merely the preamble of adult productivity in a meritocratic society' (2017, p. 13). The addition of neuroscientific ideas to human capital theory in early childhood is a response to the 'shifting problems of the neoliberal state' (Millei and Joronen 2016, p. 389). The neuroscientific narrative has an 'inseparable twin brother' in the form of the social investment state, while the idea that the individual is entirely responsible for their failures and successes is 'silently and gradually accepted' (Vandenbroeck and Olsson 2017, p. 86). Poverty is forgotten as a structural problem and reduced to an 'adverse childhood experience' (as discussed further later). This wider political project of the maintenance of neoliberalism through the adoption of new knowledges such as neuroscience (McGimpsey et al 2017) cannot be ignored as a broader underlying theme to this discussion. The incursion of the 'new neuros' into the political sphere is symptomatic for some of 'neuromolecular capitalism' (Pykett 2012): 'brain sciences are implicated in flexible capitalism; the kind of capitalism which requires emotionally intelligent, self-managing, risk-handling, relationship-managing, adaptive and entrepreneurial actors' (2012, p. 860 after Ulshöfer 2008). These alignments with political imperatives make neurosciences useful and attractive to policy makers and governments.

Finally, the 'hopeful ethos' of some neuroscience provides a final reason for its popularity. Perhaps, findings such as the idea that brains can adapt and change provide a 'transcendent "hopeful ethos" that challenges neo-liberal rationality' (see also Abi-Rached and Rose 2010; Edwards et al 2015, p. 168). Perhaps the gains of neuroscience and other biological developments could be put to work in the name of social justice, through a new 'productive interaction' of these academic fields (Youdell 2017, p. 1274). Others, meanwhile, see the use of neuroscience, particularly in the field of social policy, as the opposite of progressive (Gillies et al 2017), or as part of a worrying revival of eugenic ideas (Gillborn 2016), as I discuss in later sections.

## The influence on discourses of ability and inequality

What then, does the influence of this messy, problematic and over-hyped field of neuroscience mean for how ability is understood? This section explores what this neuroscientific 'moment' (Pykett 2012) – a culturally and historically contingent period of time where insights about the brain hold particular sway – means for how we understand ability. It is important to note that science, and the sciences of the brain in particular, have long had a role in constructing classifications: 'The psy-sciences as a discursive formation produced and continue to produce new categories and systems of classification which are then inscribed into the everyday practices of institutional life and institutional orderings, in terms of concepts like "intelligence", "ability", "hyperactivity", "normal development", "behavioural difficulties", etc.' (Ball 2013, p. 76). Therefore I focus here on what is presented as novel in the field of neuroscience, and how this relates to changing or reinvigorated notions of ability.

As mentioned, this discussion draws on the emerging literature on biosocial education (Youdell 2017; Williamson et al 2018) as well as my own previous work with colleagues on the use of neuroscience to create new policy subjects. Biosocial analysis 'interrogates the folding together of the social, cultural, biographical, pedagogic, political, affective, neurological, and biological in the interactive production of students and learning' (Youdell 2017, p. 1273). Building on an interest in embodiment in education, Youdell argues that the engagement of sociologists of education with the biological (particularly epigenetics as well as the neurosciences) should not be prevented by the abuse of these sciences by the media and policy makers. Proponents of this interdisciplinary interaction are mindful of the dangers and dangerous history of biology in education, related in particular to the use of science to justify processes with raced, gendered and ableist outcomes – the 'old threats in new, shiny technologies' (Gulson and Baker 2018 after Gillborn 2016). However they argue that there is a need to take seriously the proliferation of bio discourses, including their potential to 'provide another avenue into justice moves' (Gulson and Baker 2018, p. 160). I remain sceptical as to the possibilities of disruption through scientific discourses given the history of biology and inequality; science is always '*inside* culture' (Connor and Ferri 2007, p. 39, emphasis in original), after all. However, here I attempt to take on board this call to engage with new biological rationalities in education (and early years), by considering in depth the relationship between a neuro-imagining of the child as brain, and the reproduction of inequality.

In the following I set out two ways in which I see the new brain sciences as reinforcing and reinvigorating claims about innate and determined levels of ability and their relation to social class, and to a lesser extent, minoritised groups. First, I consider the ways in which a recourse to the brain facilitates a conception of ability as biological, and second, I explore how the discourses of damaged brains present in policy re-inscribe conceptions of the brain as determined by social class. Embedded within these arguments is the point that the brain scan – and particularly the image of the brain as varying in size – operates as a tool for the reproduction of the idea of fixed ability, much as the IQ test has operated historically.

## The biological/psychological connection

Neuroscience and the discourses relating to its public promotion raise the 'spectre of the brain' (Marks 2016) in schools, highlighting the biological and psychological facets of a child as learner. This is 'neurological foundationalism with a specific organological locus' (Baker 2015, p. 171), whereby children are reduced to brains. To put it simply, these ideas about brains remind us of the biological nature of the human – the physicality of the brain as object – and draw attention to the differences between them, while making these differences seem natural and inevitable. As I argued previously (Bradbury 2013b), the early years of education operate within a different set of discourses relating to ability, where the biological connection between brain and attainment is more apparent. Although this sector is not my focus here, it is useful to think about how the young age of children makes these connections more palatable, within the broader context of education.

In early years, the term 'development' is often used alongside, or instead of, 'ability'. Children are described within policy documentation as having a 'Good Level of Development' or not, while the language of progress along pre-defined steps in various curriculum areas forms the basis of the curriculum (DfE c). In earlier research, I found such frequent slippage between the terms ability and development that I referred to it as a hybrid concept. I argued then that 'the pseudo-scientific overtones of "development" give the term "ability" a neutrality and inevitability that is usually only alluded to ... The result of this entwinement is a potent and dangerous conception of ability/development as measurable and neutral' (Bradbury 2013b, p. 69). This is relevant here in that I would argue that neuroscience brings that neutrality and pseudo-scientific legitimacy to 'ability' in the rest of education beyond early years. Drawing on longer-standing discourses from psychology, the new use of neuroscience reinvigorates the biological relationship between brain and what a child can or cannot achieve:

> there is a danger that neuroscientific discourse is infiltrating education in order to merely reproduce in a different guise the inner personality of theory and assessment practices already embedded in existing psychological discourse in education. Technological developments may be breathing

new life into old practices and merely continue to locate deficit in the form of inadequate and incomplete representations of individual young people. (Billington 2017, pp. 869–70)

One example of these connections between the old and the new arose in the Grouping Project, where some teachers described their reasoning for dividing children in the nursery class based on their phonics skills:

'They all start in Phase 1 and then when they're ready, the would move into Phase 2 … you would do little games and things with them in amongst Phase 1 and see if they were able to do them or pick them up. So you might play like "I spy" games, you know, can they hear the initial sound in the word and then you know that they're ready and if they can't, if you say, "I spy, something beginning with 'K'" and they say "Lamppost" then you know that they haven't got any clue. … So things like can they listen out for sounds if they're not at a point where the can hear environmental sounds and know what they are then they're definitely not ready to move out of Phase 1.' (Nursery Teacher, Moore Primary)

'So you have some children who already know all their sounds and everything like that, where you have other children who still can't hear a sound so it's very difficult to teach those children together.' (School Leader, Whiteread Primary)

Here some children are physically able (or developed enough) to 'hear' the sounds, while others are not. This means that some children can move on to the next phase of learning sounds, becoming Phase 2 children, while others cannot. This 'hearing' is presented as biological or developmental, rather than a skill which is culturally and discursively situated; the familiarity of sounds in English is dependent on hearing standard English regularly. But some of these skills are also linked to 'different experiences'; for example, the learning of nursery rhymes is related to the ability to hear standard sounds in English, and the playing of games such as 'I spy' is also dependent on familiarity with similar games. The slippages between these biological and social distinctions between children are potentially dangerous, reproducing differences between children as simultaneously natural *and* determined by background, often in confused ways. As Hayes et al argue, 'One of the concerns when biological insights lead to explanations of a lack of motivation or low school achievement, with no connection to social and cultural insights, is the re-inscription of discourses about the normal' (2018, p. 184).

There were also examples from this project of teachers talking about children's "deficits" affecting their group placement (Year 2 Teacher, Hepworth Primary). Others spoke of the naturalness of some children's abilities, while also mentioning different backgrounds:

> 'if they've got a natural flair for mathematics, you have to really give them the opportunities to explore that. … They choose [activities] because it's their natural ability. So children are all very different. Some children come to school and they're just ready to go while other children just need a lot of nurturing to get to that point. … If you had all the children come to school at the same point and everybody's brains were the exact same but it's not.' (School Leader, Whiteread Primary)

We see here how the differences in children's brains are described as 'natural' and therefore unchangeable; some children are 'ready to go' and others not. As Billington comments:

> Given the power of discourses relating to intelligence and hereditability and given also the ways in which they continue to justify many forms of educational and social exclusion, caution is understandable when contemporary governments are similarly seduced by the claims of a new sciences which promise finally to reveal simple biological 'truths' about learning behaviour and education with 'neuro-' replacing or re-invigorating the old 'pyscho-'. (Billington 2017, p. 869)

One of the 'simple biological truths' that is re-inscribed through application of neuroscience to education is the popular trope of 'bigger brain = more intelligence'. There is a danger that this is reawakened by images of the brain from scans, with resulting links to perceptions of difference between social groups or genders; the risk is that an 'uncritical use of new imaging technology may open the door to a new kind of old fashioned phrenology' (Bao and Pöppel 2012, p. 2144, cited in Billington 2017, p. 874) referring to the discredited study of the shape and size of the cranium as an indicator of abilities. The

OECD report on neuroscience warns against such determinism and 'early labelling and exclusion', citing a proposal in France in 2005 to screen three-year-old brains for potential behaviour disorders at age 15 (OECD 2008, p. 129). These connections between ability and biology are symptomatic of what Abi-Rached and Rose call the 'neuromolecular gaze', described as a 'particular style of thought' and 'a common vision of life itself' based on a molecular understanding of the brain (2010, pp. 11, 13). For others, the novelty of neuroscience belies continuities with established ideas: 'the fact that terms and concepts from neuroscience and genetics exist within policy reports or the accounts of those who develop new services does necessarily imply fundamentally new kinds of social praxis. Rather novel articulations of the imagined biological potentially reify policy paths already mapped or trod' (Pickersgill 2018, p. 104).

Similarly, Baker explains 'I am extremely concerned about the recirculation of racializing, sexualizing, and ableizing tendencies in such [neuroscience] literature and the prospect of neugenics – the "backdoor" to a new version of the seemingly ideal child' (2015, p. 172). Philosophical critiques have drawn comparisons with even older concepts: Kitchen decries neuroscience as 'nothing more than a modernized materialist version of ill-fated and problematic seventeenth century mentalist philosophy' in his extended critique (2017, p. 2). But, however we understand these shifts and commonalities, it is clear that there is potential for neuroscience to biologise our conception of the child and their educational and social trajectory; bringing the brain into the equation enlivens the conception of ability as innate, in potentially dangerous ways.

### The irreparable brain

One issue remains unresolved in this discussion: how can ideas from neuroscience, which emphasise the interrelation of genetics and environment, be reconciled with the idea of intelligence as fixed and inheritable? Surely these ideas can be used, as suggested in some hopeful texts, to challenge the old orthodoxies of hierarchically ordered human beings? I would argue this is possible, and I hope this comes to pass; however, at present, we see the influence of ideas about environment and brains having a more pernicious effect, which serves to reproduce social inequalities. While we have seen examples of how recourse to the brain reproduces the idea of ability as innate, in this section I discuss how these same ideas are used to argue that brains *depend on backgrounds*. I return to the tensions between these strands later on.

In education and social policy, neuroscience has been used to justify 'early intervention' into poorer children's lives, with the aim of reducing the damage inflicted on their brains (Gillies et al 2017; McGimpsey et al 2017). The series of Early Intervention reports from the CSJ in the late 2000s and early 2010s used pictures of brain scans on their covers in simplistic ways (Allen and Smith 2008; Allen 2011b). As mentioned, 'insights' from neuroscience relating to the importance of the early years were used to explain the necessity of intervening in some families' lives, producing these families as sites of policy urgency. For example, scientific 'facts' are presented such as: 'a newborn's brain is quarter the size of an adult's, whereas by age three, it is 80 per cent formed' (Allen 2011b, p. 56). These reports are examples of the 'optimisation' discourse of neuroscience, whereby 'an implicit or explicit imperative is presented for individuals to meet their potential and to help others achieve theirs' (Broer and Pickersgill 2015b, p. 56).

In the Early Intervention reports, findings about environment and the brain are related to 'deficits' and lower IQs:

> children exposed to chronic and unpredictable stress – a parent who lashes out in fury; an alcoholic who is kind one day and abusive the next – will suffer deficits in their ability to learn. As a result, their IQs will be lower; in itself, a risk factor for conduct problems. (Allen and Smith 2008, p. 60)

These arguments present a 'montage of familiarity and novelty that has stimulated investment' (Pickersgill 2018, p. 103), combining new insights with established concerns about the impact of parenting. The original researchers whose work is used in these reports criticised the CSJ, arguing they 'greatly misrepresented' and 'distorted' findings based on children who had suffered extreme neglect in applying them to children brought up in poverty (Lewis and Bosely 2010). The idea that children are determined in their behaviours and 'ability to learn' by their environmentally affected brains has been critiqued as a form of 'neuroessentialism', where outcomes are embedded in brain processes (Rose and Rose 2012, pp. 270–1).

These ideas have been taken on at the highest levels of government: a 2016 speech by David Cameron, then prime minister, referred to the development of synapses before age two, meaning that 'Destinies can be altered for good or ill in this window of opportunity', and 'mums and dads literally build babies' brains' (Cameron, 2016, cited in Pickersgill 2018, p. 102). Importantly, these neuroscientific findings have been simplified to mean that the state must intervene in order to prevent the damage to young children's brains caused by poverty and poor parenting. This is an example of 'optimisation based on normalisation', whereby policy is a 'correction' based on predictive intervention (Gulson and Webb 2018). This discourse is then used to justify parenting policies, aimed largely at mothers (Edwards et al 2015) and even the removal of children from their families for permanent adoption (White and Wastell 2017). Neuroscience is used in discussions of 'intergenerational transmission', where parenting quality is related to adults' own childhoods: 'The implication is that today's "bad" parents act in this way as their brains were not developed properly, and thus they cannot be expected to raise their children adequately unless interventions can override "fixed" biological constraints' (Lowe et al 2015b, p. 18).

As mentioned, in Edwards et al's study of how policy makers and practitioners use neuroscience in their work, respondents identified the Early Intervention reports, and particularly the brain scan images, as influential in their decision making and levels of motivation. As one respondent explained, a photo of a brain scan provided a source of motivation (Edwards et al 2015, p.180). The use of the 'damaged brain' image (which relates to a child who suffered extreme and severe neglect) on the cover of one of the CSJ reports powerfully establishes a divide between the 'good brain' of the child with supportive (and affluent) parents, and the 'bad/small/damaged brain' of the child in poor circumstances. The image has spread much further beyond the original report. There are implicit judgements made within these documents about the causes of these circumstances: 'early intervention using brain science claims essentialises mother-child relations, biologises ideas about cycles of deprivation and reproduces classed value judgements about the means of achieving the "right sort" of brain development' (2015, p. 168). Women are held responsible for their children's brain development, required to 'invest time and positive emotional connection in their children as an intense self-managed project – the success of which can be captured in baby brain scan images' (2015, p. 177). Policy is justified by the assertion that 40 per cent of British babies not attached securely to their parents, for instance in a Sutton Trust report (Moullin et al 2014, p. 9), though the parameters of secure attachment or how this is established are not discussed. The pressure of secure attachment happens even before birth, representing 'the shift to an actuarial society within which women are held responsible for the outcome of pregnancy' (Lowe et al 2015b, p. 26).[1] Brain science claims lead to anxiety and guilt among parents, particularly middle-class parents, who are concerned they are not parenting their child 'correctly'; they are a methods of responsibilising citizens (Broer and Pickersgill 2015b, p. 54).

Interestingly, ideas from neuroscience are seen by some as challenging the social class-based hierarchies of education; Frank Field, the Labour MP, states in Edwards et al's study, '[Brain science] breaks the class spell' (2015, p. 181). Perhaps in this new neuro-world anyone can be anything, if you work hard enough. However, the impact of these ideas on practitioners and policy makers appears to have an opposite effect, instead reintroducing discourse which remind us of the 'feeble-minded' poor child, beyond education. As Millei and Joronen argue, 'it [neuroscience] has led to eugenic arguments by re-inscribing social and economic differences into differences in brain architecture' (Millei and Joronen 2016, p. 389). The idea that ability is fixed and innate by the time a child arrives at school (though there is some continuing external influence) is made acceptable and scientific by these brain-based explanations. As I discuss further later, the use of neuroscience in policy related to young children in the UK has parallels in Australian policy, where neuroscience is described as proving that 'the first five years last a lifetime' (Millei and Joronen 2016, p. 397, citing report by Winter). Similar concerns about disadvantaged children's brains being 'pruned too early' have been described as 'technologies of anticipation', in that they are policies based on future risk and prediction (2016, p. 396).

We cannot be sure of the influence of these ideas of damaged and differently sized brains on teachers in schools without research on this specific question. What is clear, from the descriptions of 'ability' discussed in Chapter 2, is that some teachers see background as having influenced ability. Some children are described as having more skills and independence than others; others are described in the previous section as 'ready to go' when they first arrive. These differences are linked to backgrounds and experiences; what the then Secretary of State for Education called the 'last taboo' of the 'home learning environment' (HLE) (Hinds 2018). This connection is also present in discussion of the 'vocabulary gap' between children, which is suggested to be 4,000 words by the age of seven (Bromley 2018; DfE 2018). The resulting discussion of 'word rich' and 'word poor' children, and the implications of 'vocabulary deficiency' or 'stunted vocabularies' (Adams 2018; OUP 2018) is inevitably related to home exposure to words, along class lines.

These assumptions were brought to the fore more publicly during the first lockdown period of the COVID-19 pandemic in the UK, as discussions of the comparable experiences of disadvantaged children and their peers while unable to attend school focused on differential parental expectations and capacity. This reductionism has potential to create simple divides between the child who can learn and the child who is challenging, based on differences between a 'normal' HLE and a deficient one, or a vocabulary-rich environment. This is part of the *biologisation* of parenting (Lowe et al 2015a), where how mothers and fathers choose to behave is seen as irreparably affecting the child. This kind of deterministic interpretation 'leaves little capacity for children to be considered as autonomous individuals who are active agents in their own lives' (Lowe et al 2015b, p. 19); it also tends to be focused far more on the disadvantaged mother than on a middle-class one. The 'tendency of the technology is towards normalcy' and revealing of brains which are otherwise (Billington 2017, p. 875); however, I would agree with Billington's view that 'It would be a serious educational, psychological and indeed serious scientific error were we to ignore the void that exists between compelling images of electrical activity in the brain and the actual experience of persons which remain much less accessible to any form of neurological or psychological reductionism' (2017, pp. 875–6).

To illustrate the dangers of this form of reductionism, I turn now to the recent growth of 'trauma-informed practice' in education.

There has always been a huge commercial sector which attempts to persuade schools that they require their products and training, and neuroscience provides a foundation for many new 'essential' products and training programmes. This has taken the form of 'brain gym' and neuro-linguistic programming in the UK, but a more recent trend internationally has been the promotion of 'trauma-informed practice' (see Mayor 2018 for an overview). This set of ideas is premised on the idea that 'professionals must understand the impact of trauma on child development and learn how to effectively minimise its effects without causing more trauma', as described by the US Department of Health and Human Services (Child Welfare Information Gateway n.d.). This principle, that some children will need to be treated differently based on their 'adverse childhood experiences' (ACEs), resonates with the damaged-brain hypothesis which dominates the Early Intervention reports in the UK. There are tests which result in 'ACE scores', itself an apparently deterministic model where children cannot escape their environment, even if professionals seek to alleviate it. US government publications such as 'Supporting Brain Development in Traumatized Children and Youth' focus on screening, and also on recovery, for trauma-affected children. I am not arguing here that this work is not helpful or well meaning, but instead my point is that these descriptions of ways of working with older children, which understand their brains to have been adversely affected by trauma, show a way of understanding the child as *based on their brain*. Notably, ACEs include various forms of abuse, alcohol or drug dependence in the home, parental separation, and imprisonment of a household member (BBC News 2018).

Training in trauma-informed practice is available for professionals in medical and social care fields, and the organisation 'Trauma Informed Schools' in the UK provides training for schools. They describe their work as preventing the development of mental health problems and their 'inventions' as 'evidence based with the backing of over 1000 research studies from psychology and neuroscience' (Trauma Informed Schools n.d.). Their slogan is 'We need to catch these children as they are falling not after they have fallen'. One whole-school training session offered includes as a first point: 'The neuroscience and psychology of child and adolescent mental health and mental ill-health: what every teacher needs to know' (TIS n.d.). On their site there is a link to an article in *SEN* magazine written by 'neuroscience expert' Dr Margot Sunderland, which exemplifies the use of brain science in relation to children in this field: 'Symptomology of ADHD and several other common child diagnoses is very similar to that of childhood trauma and loss ... Research shows that traumatised children often have the same over-activation in a key detecting threat system in their brain (the amygdala) as soldiers coming back from war-torn countries' (Sunderland n.d.). These quite extreme comparisons between trauma-affected child brains and soldiers' brains (though backed up by citations) again open up a divide between normal and abnormal; educable and uneducable. Neuroscience, including scientific terms, is used to explain some children's behaviours. Misunderstandings of children's behaviour, Sunderland argues, can be significant: case studies are described where decisions such as removing a child from their mother are criticised because 'no one had done any neuroscience homework'.

There are clear resonances with the conclusions drawn in the Early Intervention reports. The two areas were indeed combined in a November 2018 report from the House of Commons Science and Technology Committee titled 'Evidence-based Early Years Intervention' (HoC Science and Technology Committee 2018). The report discusses the correlation between adverse experiences and later 'negative consequences' and is cautious in its approach, noting that correlation is not causation and the views of neuroscientists that our understanding is still limited. However, the text later states 'Although neuroscience cannot yet say with certainty how ACEs might cause negative outcomes, there is strong evidence to suggest that brain development is affected by external factors, and that the early years are a critical period for development with consequences that can last throughout life' (2018, p. 15). Thus, neuroscience remains a powerful strategy for the justification of early intervention programmes based on ACEs, which are the main focus of the report. In a summary section, there are calls for a new strategy which 'should also recognise the scope for improved awareness of the importance of adverse early years experiences on child development, and knowledge of the latest science in this domain, across the early years workforce' (2018, p. 4). Throughout these discussions, we see again how disadvantage is 're-positioned as a biological phenomenon' (White and Wastell 2017, p. 46), and the divide between the normal and the damaged brain, dependent on family life, is established as scientific fact. The myth of the first three years justifies the focus on young children, while the wider context of families is ignored in the construction of ACE scores. A further example from the US of this kind of class-based brain discourse comes from Busso and Pollack's discussion of workshops for education professionals titled 'Enriching the Brains of Students in Poverty', which covers the 'four ways the brains of kids from poverty are physically different' and linked solutions (2015, p. 177).

The example of trauma-informed practice illustrates the strength of the influence of neuroscience and how these ideas can reinforce social inequalities by encouraging professionals to view children's brains as inevitably different. Neuroscience provides a narrative which underlies the concept of ability used in schools and the social inequalities that result. This is a discourse which links clearly to the focus on poorer families in the early years; this entire edifice 'relies on a meritocratic construction of the wealthy and privileged as having better developed brains' (Edwards et al 2015, p. 184). There is a complex combination of fixedness and plasticity at work here, representing a tension which is also seen in popular representation of the brain as 'hard-wired' and neuroscience's focus on plasticity (Youdell 2017, p. 1278). Here we also see the influence of epigenetics, as a new version of 'soft inheritance' (Meloni 2017), where parental influence is regarded as vitally important. In this discourse, genes are fixed, but the environment affects how they are activated and develop, meaning that the children can be understood as arriving at school with determined paths which are simultaneously innate and affected by background. Moreover, there is also a risk that such discourses may affect how students think of themselves and their levels of agency (Busso and Pollack 2015; Mayor 2018), a suggestion that requires further empirical research in this era where a neoliberal discourse of self-improvement through a positive 'growth mindset' abounds (TES 2017; Bradbury 2019c).

In the era of COVID-19, the language of trauma among children returned to the fore as various organisations offered training for teachers on dealing with pupils traumatised by the pandemic (NEU 2020; The National College 2020). Neuroscientists and psychologists publicly called for a 'release' from lockdown for children and young people, due to concerns about the impact on their mental health, arguing that school closures would damage the 'mental resilience and educational preparedness' they would need when entering adulthood in a period of recession (Roxby 2020).

We can also see more sinister implications for the kind of discourses reproduced in the Early Intervention reports and the literature around trauma-informed practice. Based on their analysis of the use of neuroscience in Australian early childhood policy, Millei and Joronen warn that 'these forms of reasoning also produce particular lives as worthy of securing "valued life" and those who could be abandoned as "surplus life"' (Mitchell 2009, cited in Millei and Joronen 2016, p. 396). Echoing Judith Butler's discussion of 'grievable life' (2010), they note the risk that predictions of future capability based on the idea of damaged brains could limit where spending is focused, creating a division between 'those who had gained proper neurological childhood and thus have a value, a human capital, for Australia's race in global competition, and to those who had not' (2016, p. 400). This echoes the 1960s crisis of the 'disadvantaged child' in the US, where 'surplus populations became determined and demarcated, as early as three years old' (Jackson 2014, p. 190). The gold bar illustration on the Early Intervention report, in this context, provokes the question, what should the state do with the child with the smaller brain? Are they part of the 'surplus' population? We have already seen policy on SureStart Children's Centres influenced by the 'progressive eugenics' of Dominic Cummings, then an aide in the Department of Education (Tomlinson 2019); potentially other aspects of early years provision could be affected by policy aimed at children who have not had a 'proper neurological childhood'.

## The 'damaged brain' and race

Before I conclude this chapter, it is worth acknowledging that this discussion has focused on the significance of social class in descriptions of how brains differ. This is not to say, however, that the historical significance of brains and their relative sizes in different communities has been ignored. Perhaps, as Penn argues in relation to the use of neuroscience in international development work, 'it is possible to argue that poverty and low income have replaced race as a marker of inadequacy, and poverty is a signal that intervention is necessary, as race once was' (Penn 2017, pp. 60–1). It would not be acceptable to talk of different sized brains related to 'racial origin', she comments, but reports from UNICEF and the World Bank explain how neuroscience can help 'the world's most disadvantaged children' (UNICEF 2014, p. 1, cited in Penn 2017, p. 56). Similarly, in domestic policy, we have seen earlier how the focus on the ambiguously defined 'disadvantaged' child can be justified through neuroscience in ways which are at times, implicitly racialised, particularly where this only one model of 'good parenting' which is implicitly based on white middle-class norms: 'Applying a scientised logic of early intervention positions some cultures at greater risk of genetic impairment and brain damage simply because of their childreading practices. The implications of this reasoning range from a sanctioning of culturally insensitive professional practice to a potential resurgence of biologised racism' (Edwards et al 2015, p. 180). This is certainly an area which requires further exploration and research, given the long history of links between the brain and racism discussed in previous chapters.

As discussed, one of the main concerns of those writing about the discourses of educational neuroscience has been that it essentialises groups of pupils and may 'be used to justify social inequalities' (Busso and Pollack 2015, p. 175), including racial inequalities. In Australian policy based on neuroscience, 'Racist exclusion enters into this constellation, ... not as a necessity but as a breaking point and logical counterpart of the biological improvement in the population' (Millei and Joronen 2016, p. 399). Race has never been far away from discussions of brains, and the context of the new geneism (Gillborn 2016) or new eugenics (Baker 2015) provides fertile ground for racist associations between damaged brains, backgrounds, and differential social and educational outcomes.

## Conclusion

In this chapter I have explored how the 'new neuros', fields of scientific enquiry centred around the brain, have become part of the assemblage of influences on policy and practice, translated into everyday language and simplified in potentially problematic ways. The hype around neuroscience in education – the 'neuroturn' – has led to the re-inscription of old established ideas of ability as innate, both through providing simple reminders of the biological nature of difference, and through a conceptualisation of children's brains as either damaged by their early years or not. This all takes places within a neoliberal context where human capital theory underpins much policy making: we must remember that, as in the Australian case, 'neuroscientific rationalizations … have not emerged in an empty space, but in a space that has been occupied by previous biopolitical understandings of human capital' (Millei and Joronen 2016, p. 390). Thus the use of neuroscience represents not a fundamental alteration, but 'more of a shift *within* biopolitical government that leads to new categorizations and forms of discrimination based on biological and naturalizing arguments' (Millei and Joronen 2016, p. 390; see also McGimpsey et al [2017] on the extent of alterations to the neoliberal subject).

A key point here is that how we currently think about what children can do, what is 'normal' and what is not, and how children compare is influenced profoundly by the reification of the physical brain as a symbol of broader 'ability'. In this process, the brain scan image becomes the visual manifestation of the difference between people, a seemingly objective snapshot of how different we can be, in much the same way as the IQ test before it. The image of the brain has become the signifier of scientific authority, symbolic of fundamentally different brain types which we can assess and treat/teach differently. Significantly, one of the main contributions of neuroscience so far appears to be that children's brains are affected by their backgrounds; this is a step backwards which perpetuates unequal outcomes, and a revival of a dangerous discourse of labelling and determinism.

For many involved in the emerging field of critical neuroscience, the project is to remind us that 'neuroscience itself as a cultural activity' (Choudhary et al 2009, p. 63, cited in Pykett 2012, p. 859). It shapes our understanding of what it is to be human (Billington 2017). In Foucauldian terms, it provides another biopolitical frame through which the population can be assessed and controlled. Children can be classified through their brains, not only by measures such as IQ, but by assessments of the 'damage' done to them as infants, which has affected them permanently; this is a biopolitics which reaches into our very heads to ascertain our usefulness.

In the next chapter, I return to the idea of testing and discuss how the production of data and the reverence with which they are held also have an impact on ability and inequality.

# 5

# Data and the solidification of ability

## Introduction

In this chapter, I explore the impact of a second educational trend which sees an increased emphasis placed on data about children within schools, known as *datafication*. As with neuroscience, I begin with a discussion of the role of data in education, before considering the relation to concepts of ability and to the reproduction of inequalities. The field of data and education is vast and written about extensively elsewhere (for example, Eynon 2013; Lingard and Sellar 2013; Selwyn et al 2015; Lupton and Williamson 2017) so I provide an overview of the main debates and points of discussion, before focusing specifically on the relationship between data and concepts of ability. I wish to emphasise the ways in which current data-focused practices work to reinforce long-standing ideas about children as positioned on a *spectrum of ability*, where they can be compared with each other. These positions are solidified through data and as such lead to deterministic predictions of what children can or cannot do, as exemplified through the drift towards measurements of progress over raw attainment.

Through this chapter I discuss the impact of data on values, as well as on practice. A datafied education system is one governed by a specific rationality, whereby numbers become the means through which we understand children and their potential, but also the teacher's worth and impact. Like others, I argue that a datafied education system can exclude other ways of thinking about value in education, while appearing common-sense; Lingard and Sellar, for example, note the 'naturalisation of data as the most sensible medium for thinking about teaching and learning' (2013, p. 652); meanwhile Popkewitz comments that 'it is almost impossible to think about schooling without numbers' (2012, p. 169). This 'tyranny of numbers' (Ball 2015) as a way of understanding what matters in education – like the concept of ability, a regime of truth – shapes priorities, practices and the operation of power.

Before I turn to how data are used and datafication in education, it is worth noting that the increased prominence of data is a phenomenon present in many sectors – what has been called the 'data deluge' (Kitchin

2014, p. xv) – and there is much positivity around the potential for Big Data to change society and government (Eynon 2013). In some education sectors this also applies, for example, where data are seen as a new means of transparency. In the era of COVID-19, the growth of online learning as schools were closed further solidified the role of technology in education, establishing 'the digital as the "magic" to remake education' (Grimaldi et al 2020). Given the inextricable link between data production and digital technology (Selwyn 2016a), this suggests the trend in the immediate future will be towards more data production, though perhaps of different types; teachers may be monitoring students' interaction levels as much as attainment data, perhaps. Overall, however, most of the critical work focuses on the dangers of data, and on the problems of a sector 'drowning in data' but ill-equipped to make use of them (Roderick 2012). I begin with a discussion of how and why data have multiplied in schools.

## The growth of data in schools

In 2018 the Secretary of State for Education commissioned a report into schools' use of data as part of an attempt to tackle teacher workload; one conclusion was that 'Data is often used too much for monitoring and compliance, rather than to support pupil learning and school improvement. This audit culture can lead to feelings of anxiety and burnout in staff' (Teacher Workload Advisory Group 2018, p. 4). This reflects the broader concerns expressed by teachers about the ways in which schools have become over-reliant on data, or 'data-obsessed' as I have put it elsewhere (Bradbury and Roberts-Holmes 2017c), to the detriment of teaching and learning. The impact of data production on workload and retention has also become a political focus (ATL 2016). In primary schools, the removal of National Curriculum levels had a particularly significant impact as schools were left to recalibrate their methods of assessing attainment and progress, while still under pressure to 'perform' in standardised tests such as the SATs tests at age 10/11 (Year 6) (Bradbury 2019d; Pratt and Alderton 2019). The labels of Level 3, 4 and 5 which had dominated many Year 6 teachers' lives for so long were replaced with a scaled score of between 80 and 120, with 100 as the 'expected standard' to be used in school performance measures. Progress measures were also changed, to add to the complexity, while there were new rules for assessing 'floor' standards, the minimum schools must achieve to avoid increased inspection and scrutiny. During the same period of the 2010s, primary schools also had to respond to reformed versions of the EYFSP and Key Stage 1 SATs, and the introduction of the Phonics Screening Check in Year 1, and latterly, the Multiplication Tables Check in Year 4. All of these statutory assessments produce data, and in turn encourage the production of more monitoring data between tests. The abandoned introduction of Baseline Assessment for Reception Children in 2015, and again in 2019 (where the plan to make it statutory in autumn 2020 was cancelled due to the pandemic) further exemplified this process of datafication, where the measurement of 'value added' by schools had prominence (Roberts-Holmes et al 2020). As these changes came as part of the 'policy storm' of initiatives from the Coalition Government, they provoked a range of responses, including a return to greater grouping by ability (Bradbury 2018b). Research suggests teachers' responses to the loss of established National Curriculum levels were often to adopt 'something akin to levels but alternatively named'; as one teacher cited commented, 'it is so embedded in people's practice to think of a child as being at a numerical value' (Pratt and Alderton 2019, p. 588). Pratt and Alderton also found, reflecting the comments from the Teacher Workload Advisory Group discussed earlier, that assessment data operated as much as systems of scrutiny as for planning learning; one teacher commented 'We just need something to make up a story with and it [assessment data] is providing that'. Primary schools rely on data to show their worth, and as such, the production, discussion and monitoring of data have become key tasks and levers.

In secondary education, changes to assessment included the renaming of grades at GCSE to 1–9, and changes to value added measures used in performance tables. Schools are assessed on the proportion of students gaining a Grade 5 in English and Maths, and their EBacc results, which show the proportion of students getting Grade 5 or higher in English, maths, combined science (two GCSEs), history or geography and a language. League tables also include the Progress 8 score, which uses Key Stage 2 SATs data (from the last year of primary school tests) compared to GCSE results to measure the 'value added' by the school based on prior attainment (DfE 2016). The eight subjects included are English and maths (which are double weighted), combined science, history or geography and a language, plus the three highest-scoring additional subjects for each student. Schools are also judged on their Attainment 8 scores, which measure raw attainment in these subjects. The complexity of these measures and their predictive nature (calculating students' expected GCSE grades from their SATs results) engenders the production of data.

## The datafication of education

The term datafication, used widely in commercial contexts and first applied to education by Lingard et al (2013), can be broadly defined in terms of the increased prominence of data in education. Technological innovation and societal expectations about the potential of this new technology to improve education have led to data having an increased importance and prominence in the everyday operation of schools (Bradbury and Roberts-Holmes 2017c). In this context, 'data' has a wide-ranging definition, including biographical information on pupils, observational information on their behaviour and conduct, measures and predictions of progress, and of course, most numerously, attainment data. These attainment data may be numbers, levels and sub-levels, grades or colour-coded statements, all of which are compared against set benchmarks for age-related expected levels and for expected rates of progress between set points. These data are essential to schools' functioning, providing information during Ofsted inspections (Bradbury and Roberts-Holmes 2017a) and justifications for practice, including grouping systems (Francis et al 2019; Towers et al 2020).

As I wrote with my colleague:

> It is helpful to think about how data is produced from multiple sources and has multiple forms in classrooms, how it is transferred from one site to another and with whose permission, who has the power to alter it, and of course who controls how it is processed and delivered back to serve some purpose. (Bradbury and Roberts-Holmes 2017c, p. 6)

Datafication can be understood as 'the rendering of myriad forms of information about education, in particular about learning' (Macgilchrist 2019, p. 78) into what Williamson (2014) has termed 'machine-readable' education. Manolev et al define it as 'the conversion of social action into quantifiable data in a manner that enables the tracking of people in real-time', also noting the 'role of power within the datafication process' (2019, p. 36). I have also defined datafication as 'a shift in what can be thought, or regimes of truth, in Foucault's terms, about what matters in education' (Bradbury and Roberts-Holmes 2017c). The argument overall then seems to be that datafication is about a change in what is important, with resulting changes in what people do, who they are, and who wields power.

Underlying the range of scholarship on datafication is a critique of the objectivity and neutrality of data, and the means of its production, which is itself derived from Science and Technology Studies (STS) as well as sociology. This critique focuses on the socially contingent production of data: as Gitelman and Jackson comment, there is no such thing as 'raw' data; it is always produced in ways which reflect social relations and matrices of power (2013, p. 5). Moreover, data have a power which goes beyond their production, shaping relations and practices. Jarke and Breiter explain:

> data do not provide a 'window' to the social world, but rather the relationship between data and what they are meant to represent is recursive: Data are not 'natural' by-products of social actions, but must always be understood in the context of their origin and the affordances of the respective digital infrastructure. The datafication of education does not only transform education but also our understanding of education, of what is understood as a 'good education', associated objectives and good practices. (2019a, p. 5)

As such, 'data in this broader sense [are] a record of something which *also does work itself*' (Bradbury and Roberts-Holmes 2017c, p. 6; emphasis in original). Attainment data, in particular, have power in rendering teachers successful or not, as Pratt and Alderton remind us: 'assessment is not, as policy tends to suggest, a neutral uncovering of pupils' ability for the purposes of teaching and accountability, but a more complex, socially-constructed activity which is important in teachers' professional lives and through which they establish and maintain their professional identity (Pratt and Alderton 2019, p. 582). Thus, as I summarise later, datafication can be seen in changes to the five Ps: pedagogy, practice, priorities, people and power.

## The five Ps of datafication

**Pedagogy**: The need to produce data may impact on what is taught in the classroom and how: for example, there may be a greater focus on subjects more easily measured or those subjects which feature in tests (such as English and maths). There may be more time spent on testing or other assessments, reducing the time spent by the teacher interacting with children. In our research in the early years, we found teachers were distracted by the need to record children's attainments with a tablet and then allocate these to a government early learning goal (Bradbury and Roberts-Holmes 2017c). They also felt the need to design particular tasks to assess the specific skills measured in assessments.

**Practices:** First, there may be a shift in how classrooms are organised as data provide justification for systems of setting, streaming and grouping by ability. These decisions may be made through the data, rather than teacher judgement (Taylor et al 2018; Towers et al 2020), in a seemingly objective manner. At the same time, the pressures of high-stakes data, including progress data, encourage the targeting of particular children (through 'educational triage' and interventions, as discussed later) and the physical separation of pupils from one another. Secondly, datafication changes how teachers work: their role as data collectors means that a key indicator of professionalism is the keeping of extensive data and familiarity with the pertinent trends within them. Time is spent entering data, discussing them with colleagues and putting into place actions based on the stories they tell – here data 'can also be used as a legitimizer' for decisions made (Jennings 2012).

**Priorities:** Datafication produces a shift in priorities towards the production and analysis of numbers, at times to the detriment of teaching: 'producing the right second-order objectives (numbers) has become as important as first-order objectives (pedagogy, curriculum, assessment) in new performative accountability regimes' (Gulson and Sellar 2018, p. 2). This means that teacher time and effort focus on data entry and analysis, over other classroom tasks. This is seen in the shifts in pedagogy discussed earlier, where gathering data may become more important than actual teaching.

**People:** The dominance of data changes the role of teacher, school leader and pupil, as well as creating new stakeholders such as the professional data analyst (often 'bought in'). Pupils become the raw materials to be 'mined' for data, transformed into 'auditable commodities' (Keddie 2016); meanwhile teachers become recorders and facilitators of data-producing contexts, as well as assessors and consumers themselves of data visualisations (Ratner et al 2019). School leaders, in conjunction with other formal and informal analysts of the data such as professional data processing companies, school governors, trusts and, of course, Ofsted, are required to 'read' the data in particular ways, and provide an accompanying narrative (their 'Ofsted story') about the success of the school. Data-driven subjectivities mean that the child as person runs alongside their *data double*, a numerical or visual representation of them as represented in the school data – their 'data doppelgänger' (Williamson 2014). The teacher is remade as operating within a moral framework in which manipulation of the data is a logical response to pressure (Thompson and Cook 2014; Hardy 2015). This is the 'constitutive power of data, software and code' (Beer 2015, p. 3) operating in education, shaping teacher and child subjectivities to reflect the importance of data. Thus 'the process described is not simply a change to what is done and how, but also a change to *who people are*, or who they are expected to be' (Bradbury and Roberts-Holmes 2017c, p. 7; emphasis in original).

**Power:** Finally, the proliferation of data alters relations of power. At a nation-state level, data make education governable (Ozga 2009; Lingard and Sellar 2013); they are vital in neoliberal processes of accountability as a form of surveillance (or dataveillance). For example, the designation of some schools as 'coasting' by the UK government was determined by analysis of their GCSE or SATs data over the last three years. At a school level, datafication pushes professionals in certain directions (Hardy 2015; Roberts-Holmes 2015; Pratt 2016) as they are monitored through data, and subject to increased visibility. For example, a headteacher participant in Hardy's work on the impact of the national testing system in Australia expressed their strategy of 'embedding data in the mindset of teachers' (Hardy 2014, p. 9). School leaders too are subject to data demands, constituted as powerful or otherwise in their local networks based on their school's performance data (Coldron et al 2014). Furthermore, datafication invites new actors into the equations of power in schooling (Manovich 2012, 2013; Lynch 2015; Piattoeva 2015): the data analyst becomes a key interpreter and translator of a school's data, whether they be employed by the school, part of a commercial company, or 'bought in' temporarily. Private companies wield power as the controllers of large datasets on children, as software such as Tapestry or Target Tracker are sold as methods to make the processing of data easier for teachers; these companies mediate the pressure of datafication into schools by appealing to the ethos of the sector (Bradbury 2019f). Here power lies in the algorithm, or more specifically in the unknown coder who determines values within the algorithm, deciding which scores or levels of progress are classified as normal and otherwise.

This summary of the wide-ranging literature on datafication in education is my own analysis of the key areas of impact – others may see the process differently – but this schema of effects highlights the multifaceted operation of data at all levels of education. It is not an exhaustive list, and indeed the field is evolving to take into account new ways in which data affect educational processes, including those yet to come: datafication 'transforms not only the ways in which teaching and learning are organised but also the ways in which futures generations (will) construct reality with and through data' (Jarke and Breiter 2019a, p. 1).

While there is great expectation placed on the transformative power of Big Data in public discourse, the literature on data in education remains cautious. Datafication 'raises expectations ... but also associated fears' (Jarke and Breiter 2019a, p. 1): there is a trade-off to be made between greater transparency and civic participation and the dangers of surveillance and control, and the reproduction of inequalities. In education, many scholars explore concerns as to the subjectivating effects of data on students (Lupton and Williamson 2017), and the impact on the identities of teachers who may be de-professionalised by data processes (Thompson and Cook 2014). The emotional impact of digital surveillance or 'dataveillance' is another point of concern, as data make visible the 'quality' of teachers and indeed school leaders, leaving some vulnerable, while also eroding notions of trust (Ball 2003; Pratt 2016). While these broader concerns are not my main focus here, in later parts of this chapter I explore the fears raised in relation to the reproduction of inequality through datafication, particularly in relation to concepts of ability as measurable and fixed.

A set of key findings within the field of data and education is provided by the editors of a special issue on the topic. Jarke and Breiter (2019a) note that datafication:

- 'leads to new spatio-temporal entanglements and transforms translocal relationships' (2019a, p. 3);
- 'allows for and requires new forms of participation' (2019a, p. 3), such as parental engagement through behaviour monitoring, but 'these new possibilities of participation depend strongly on the respective competences to interpret data (critically) and may thus promote a new digital divide and increase inequalities' (2019a, p. 4);
- 'leads to a redistribution of agency across socio-technical networks' (2019a, p. 4); and
- 'may allow for new forms and possibilities of monitoring and surveillance' (2019a, p. 4).

These wide-ranging consequences demonstrate the breadth of work that is currently ongoing in research on data and education.

Internationally, analyses of datafication in education have focused on various different sectors, from early years to higher education, and on a variety of different levels, from the use of data in the governance of education to the role of data demands in shaping relationships in the classroom (Ozga et al 2011; Jennings 2012; Jarke and Breiter 2019a; Williamson et al 2020a). My work with Guy Roberts-Holmes in this area has focused on this local level, through an exploration of how the need to produce and analyse data affects the lives of teachers and children, as well as the school leaders and data analysts whose roles are transformed and indeed produced through accountability systems that require increasing amounts of data. Our analysis, while covering the impact of datafication on practices and priorities, has aimed to emphasise in particular the constitution of data-driven teacher and pupil subjectivities (Bradbury and Roberts-Holmes 2017c). We argue that datafication reshapes the roles of teacher as data recorder (see also Bradbury 2019f) and the children as data producers, whereby the pupils become reduced and simplified in the pursuit of greater understanding of student progress. I have argued that in early years this process of datafication is intertwined with schoolification, that is the imposition of practices and discourses used with older children into early childhood settings (Bradbury 2019b). The need to produce data results in an increased focus on maths and literacy (a key feature of schoolification) and the use of grouping by ability and interventions, as I discuss further later.

However, as noted, most recent work on datafication has focused on the operation of data at state or regional levels, and within commercial platforms, and the resulting shifts in power (Gulson and Sellar 2018; Macgilchrist 2019; Manolev et al 2019; Williamson and Piattoeva 2019). For example, Gulson and Sellar (2018) focus on the emergence of new data infrastructures in Australian education, such as the move to create consistent data systems across states. In the special issue mentioned earlier, Williamson and Piattoeva (2019) focus on the collection of data on students' social-emotional learning (SEL) as promoted by the OECD. However, despite their entirely different focus, these very different analyses of datafication offer key concepts in the analysis of the use of data more locally, I would argue, and demonstrate the evolving nature of the field.

Gulson and Sellar's focus on infrastructure and the creation of technical standards reminds us of the need to interrogate how seemingly neutral data systems are manifestations of power and products of diverse actors from both state and commercial sectors. In thinking about data use in schools, this is helpful in emphasising how the data forms collected – the boxes ticked on the spreadsheet or the boundaries of expected levels – are products of complex systems, while appearing entirely neutral. In many cases, the decision about which data are collected and how are opaque; often they combine both state and commercial actors, for example in the use of exam boards for GCSEs, which are owned by commercial companies such as Pearson.

Williamson and Piattoeva use the case study of SEL to raise some important points about the creation of objectivity through standardisation. The idea that something is fair and transparent relies on an agreement that we all test the same thing and apply the same rules; but what is often less clear is where these rules and things have come from, and where they draw their authority from. The construction of objectivity is a vital foundation for datafication, and there is a great deal of work involved in constructing this objectivity, for example through provision of exemplars of standards for national tests, which suggest standardisation (though as we see in some of the examples discussed later, teachers do not always believe in the alignment of data and the real world). Technology requires and facilitates standardisation and replicability, as seen in the example of Reception Baseline Assessment in England. The use of tablet-based tests for young children has been constructed as the only fair way to assess these young children, as teacher assessment proved too inconsistent (DfE 2017b). Thus, though an entirely different case, Williamson and Piattova's argument about policy makers' 'enduring reliance on the precarious construction of objectivity as a key legitimator of policy-relevant scientific knowledge and "evidence-based" education governance' (2019, p. 64) rings true.

Williamson's further examination of SEL (2019) emphasises the use of the data infrastructures discussed by Gulson and Sellar in the development of new policy agendas, such as the 'direct policy attention to measurements of students' behaviours and emotions' (2019, p. 1). The assembling of these data infrastructures facilitates the collection and analysis of what Williamson calls 'psychodata': 'numerical accounts of students' non-cognitive capacities', such as 'grit', 'resilience', 'growth mindset' and 'character' (2019, p. 2). These types of data present a new frontier in the datafication of education.

Finally, the continued focus on the interaction of commercial interests with educational priorities in scholarship on data and education provides further examples of the influence of networks of private companies within the sector and the complex relationship between education as a state function and private interests:

> While there nothing inherently wrong (or especially new) with these commercial contributions, questions need to be asked about regulation and oversight of corporate activities in educational settings. For example, should major 'big tech' corporations continue to exercise 'soft power' in influencing and shaping education decision-making, while all the time profiting from the decisions being made? How might we better ensure that commercial actors respond primarily to the ideals of public education rather than working to create demand for their products? (Selwyn et al 2020, p. 3)

The use of software such as Class Dojo, a 'school-based social media platform that incorporates a gamified behaviour-shaping function, providing school communities with a centralised digital network in which to interact' (Manolev et al 2019, p. 1), has been the subject of particular attention (see also Williamson 2017). Class Dojo allows for the datafication of discipline, as children score points for good behaviour, which are allocated to their own personal avatar;[1] this is an example of the SEL-informed data approaches discussed earlier.

The conditions produced by the COVID-19 pandemic provided sudden impetus to the education sector's use of technology, as thousands of children were suddenly being taught using online methods, ranging from emailed work to real-time teaching via video conferencing software. Some schools were using ClassDojo as the platform for home learning, further embedding the software into school life. During the 'pandemic politics' of the first lockdown period, 'educational technologies have been positioned as a frontline emergency service' (Williamson et al 2020b, p. 107), essential to replace the learning usually done in school. But there is a risk, Williamson et al argue, within this crisis: 'certain actors in the edtech industry are treating the crisis as a business opportunity, with potentially long-term consequences for how public education is perceived and practised long after the coronavirus has been brought under control' (Williamson et al 2020b, p. 107).

For some companies, the crisis has provided a 'great online learning experiment' (Zimmerman, 2020, cited in Williamson et al 2020b, p. 112), which might produce the evidence they require to market online learning as a suitable alternative to school or university. It has been an unprecedented opportunity to collect data: 'the pandemic can be interpreted also as global educational experiment that allowed the production of an unprecedented amount of data on the functioning of online teaching and learning' (Grimaldi et al 2020).

It seems the pandemic has great potential for further datafication of education, but perhaps in new ways, and online learning renders children 'machine readable' in new ways. Overall, the field of data and education, at all levels, brings into sharp focus and critique the underlying principles and values and the emerging power relations of datafication. I now turn to the use of data in determining practices and how this relates to concepts of 'ability'.

## Data-based ability practices

There is evidence of the processes of datafication in schools and other educational settings in England and elsewhere (Bradbury 2018a; Gulson and Sellar 2018; Jarke and Breiter 2019a), though as suggested this local-level discussion is less extensive than the literature on data-based governance (see Breiter 2016). Much of this policy-focused work builds on previous research into the practices associated with neoliberal high-stakes testing and the resulting pressures on teachers and students through regimes of performativity (Ball 2003; Perryman 2006; Keddie 2017; Holloway and Brass 2018). As such, we can see datafication as the successor to performativity, or an intensified form, as *hyper accountability*. What is emphasised, however, in recent work is the disciplinary role of data – the 'tyranny of numbers' (Ball 2015) – in shaping who teachers are, and how children can be understood. There is no longer simply a need to produce the numbers through tests, but also through ongoing assessments, tracking and predictions; moreover, the data produced on children is not simply academic, as systems of monitoring behaviour and conduct become digitised and more prevalent. One well-discussed example of this is the use of the ClassDojo app, which allows teachers to assess students' behaviour in real time, with the information relayed to parents. This normalises the surveillance of students: 'datafication and numerisation of students entices teachers with the prospect of a new and supposed efficient method of student organisation and decision-making, a governance by numbers' (Manolev et al 2019, p. 47). Thus the amassing of data goes well beyond test scores to incorporate assessments of character, resilience and grit (Williamson 2017; Williamson and Piattoeva 2019), cleanliness and self-care (Bradbury and Roberts-Holmes 2017c), and, in early years, ideas as vague as confidence, self-regulation and motivation (Bradbury 2013b). As such, the changes in the so-called three Vs of data – volume, variety and velocity (Laney, 2001, cited in Selwyn 2016a, p. 81) – particularly the volume and variety, are present in this new era of data-obsessed schools.

To illustrate some of the everyday and seemingly mundane datafied processes in play in schools in this context, here I use some new empirical data from the Grouping Project. I consider how data relate to practices which sort children into ability or attainment groups, to emphasise the very real consequences of the data/ability interaction. These data extracts provide examples of how datafication 'changes the decision-making and opinion-forming processes of education stakeholders such as education policy, school supervision, school authorities, teacher, students and parents' (Jarke and Breiter 2019a, p. 1).

Although this project was not focused on the use of data, the issue was raised repeatedly (perhaps because of my previous work on Baseline Assessment and datafication, though I doubt this work has reached many of the teachers involved). As one respondent summed up, "it's all about scores on the doors and data and targets and so on and so forth" (Focus Group 3 Participant). The pressure of assessment policy, particularly the Phonics Screening Check (PSC) in Year 1, meant that teachers who were uncomfortable with the social and emotional impact of grouping felt it to nonetheless be a 'necessary evil' (Bradbury 2018b) in order to produce 'good data'. This desire for end results was intertwined with an everyday reliance on data in making decisions; for instance, there were clear links made between the availability of attainment data and the practices of grouping:

> 'Grouping in a data driven world seems to be becoming the norm. This sadly takes away from child led play time as we are forced into writing and reading constantly rather than appreciating the real heart of EYFS.' (W)

> 'The realities of resource constraints, for example, lack of support staff and the constant fixation on data results, means that grouping becomes necessary.' (W)

Here data provide the justification and impetus for grouping, working in interaction with the concept of ability to justify why some children need to be taught separately. Processes of educational triage (Gillborn and Youdell 2000), where some children are deemed 'safe', others 'borderline' or worth working on, and others 'hopeless cases', are based on data, and we found evidence that this strategy was being used in response to pressure to improve PSC results.

> 'In Year 1 they had a panic where these children don't know these things and so then they went to a panic measure

of bringing it [grouping] in. So almost everybody was in with the teacher although it was differentiated, and then I took what was deemed, the "must get these children to pass their phonics check" group. … so they were obviously the children that they just went, "Well these ones aren't going to make it," so they're in the class doing something differentiated. Then there was the bulk going, "Yes, I think these ones are going to be fine." Then there were the other ones that they were like, "These have got to do it otherwise our score is going to be awful," basically.' (Focus Group 3 Participant)

Here decisions about prioritisation of this extra teacher are based on data, rather than children's needs, to the detriment of the 'these ones aren't going to make it' group. Thus data provide the evidence for practice, as well as motivating the strategies adopted in relation to the PSC.

Similarly, Neumann's case study research in a secondary academy found the prominence of data within the accountability regime was linked to the development of a system of 'pathways' for students, similar to streaming, which were referred to by teachers as 'top', 'middle' and 'bottom' (Neumann 2021). Although some teachers had doubts about the system, its 'data-driven character had lent it an aura of objectivity and unquestionable authority' (2021, p. 10).

In my study in primary education, data also formed the basis for interventions, which I have argued are a form of grouping which is often overlooked (Bradbury 2018b). Here small groups of children are identified and then removed from the normal class for a period to focus on one skill or area of the curriculum. In this example, a school leader describes her strategy for 'pulling out' children who have not made enough progress through the phases of phonics learning as assessed in six-weekly tests, across the year groups:

'I'm going to pull out the children who have not made much progress in early years. So those that are coming up from early years with very little phase 2 segmenting and blending going on. … So I will pull out some Year 1s, some Year 2s, possibly some newly arrived children who are actually going to be in Year 4 but they're Romanian and they haven't been here for more than a few months and they're not picking up very quickly. So although they're Year 4, they're going to really benefit from the end of phase 2 with a big push.' (School Leader, School 2)

The connection between data and ideas about ability may not be immediately clear here, but I see these practices as physical manifestations of the idea that children can be measured and organised into a hierarchy. Interventions may not label children as 'low ability' on a permanent basis, but they do define some children as 'behind' expectations, in need of remedial action. As such they form part of a discourse of division between normal and atypical children, which can been seen in the literal removal of children from he classroom[2]. Similarly, the 'hopeless case' group of pupils in systems of educational triage are labelled as not worthy of effort, and beyond teachability (Youdell 2004), because of the data they have produced so far, and the data they have the potential to produce. Children in intervention groups are failing to produce the right data too, and so are subject to particular 'practices of division' (Foucault 1977).

Together, we can see these kind of data-based practices as constituting the child through their data – the data double or data doppelgänger (Williamson 2014). The child is reduced to a number through these processes, or in some cases a colour (where green indicates meeting expectations and red suggests 'below'). This does not mean that the child is only constituted in this way – obviously their body and personality are the real substance of everyday interaction in the classroom – but that this constitution has an impact on how their real embodied self is directed to different spaces and tasks. Similarly Popkewitz (2012) has described the 'distancing' effect of numbers (in reference to Porter's work). The child as reality is separate from the child as number, reduced and 'eviscerated by enumeration' (Ball 2018). This separation has effects on what we do with numbers, so that the parallel world of data involves different ontological expectations. I return to the quote discussed in Chapter 2, where the teacher explained how interventions were used for children "who are not on track on a thingy". The teacher refers to how "you come in, all our data in your hands and literally we get names reeled off … You don't talk about the child" (Focus Group 2 Teacher). Here the child is no longer the topic of conversation, replaced by the need to record 'doing something' if a child is recorded as failing to make enough progress. The names are simply 'reeled off' based on databases of progress, and designated to interventions even if there is doubt over their impact. Interventions here become a sticking plaster over data inadequacies, providing evidence of action and attentiveness to the numbers while the child in their complexity recedes into the background. Their existence matters less than the stories that can be told about the data.

We see in these processes of datafication how powerful the quantification of children as learners can be, in reducing them to simple numbers. As Ladwig and McPherson argue: 'The presumption of a singular quantity is a function of the institutional demand for ranking, internalising and stabilising that quantity into bodies is a function of an institution that organises and regulates bodies, time and space' (2017, p. 365). Thus datafication is a biopolitical project, an engagement with the management of (school) populations, as well as having disciplinary power. It is a method of ascribing value to children which separates itself from the child as they are embodied, instead relying on standards, neutrality and objectivity as sources of authority and legitimacy. These examples provide evidence of the ways in which data operate to render difficult decisions about children neutral and non-negotiable; it is inevitable that children with lower scores (however these have been produced) will be subject to interventions or placement in lower groups. Data thus facilitate the practices of grouping by ability, while also providing an overriding motivation for the practice, which is seen as necessary to get 'good data'.

In turn we can see how the use of groups, as discussed in Chapter 2, reproduces the discourse of 'fixed ability' (Marks 2013; Drummond and Yarker 2013; Bradbury 2019e), affecting how teachers respond to the very real bodies and minds of children. Teachers' use of questions, praise and public displays of approval or disapproval have been linked to how they understand the child in terms of ability (Marks 2013). Thus the data-based practices discussed here have very real consequences which operate in symbiosis with the data themselves.

### Data and ability: the growth of progress measures

In this section I further dissect the relationship between concepts of ability and data by considering the growing use of progress measure to assess schools' performance.

Secondary schools use Progress 8, which measures the 'value added' from Key Stage 2 SATs to GCSE scores. Schools that are concerned about their Progress 8 scores inform parents of their child's expected 'flightpath' or 'pathway' through the years, and their expected grades at GCSE, and in turn, whether the child is meeting these expectations. Primary schools use measures of progress between Key Stage 1 SATs (age 6/7) and Key Stage 2 SATs (age 10/11), but there have been attempts to introduce an alternative system of assessing children on entry through Reception Baseline Assessment and using this as a starting point (this was introduced in 2015 but abandoned the year after, and a second version is in the piloting stage at the time of writing with introduction planned for 2020). This shift towards measuring progress over raw attainment – the 'reification of progress' (Bradbury and Roberts-Holmes 2017a) – has been seen by some as more sympathetic to schools where children arrive with lower attainment as it allows their impact to be recognised. However, as with all measures of 'value added' (and there have been various previous iterations), there is a risk of establishing low expectations for those with lower baselines. This is potentially dangerous if the initial assessment is affected by social and cultural factors, as in the case of Baseline Assessment in 2015 where four-year-old children with EAL received very low scores as they could not access the assessment in their home language (Bradbury 2019a). Furthermore, as discussed, research in secondaries also suggests that pupils who enter with lower scores, who as a result are not predicted to gain a passing grade at GCSE five years later, are seen as less valuable by the school and placed in different groups (Taylor-Mullings 2018).

Progress measures are an important driver of datafication in that they lend themselves to practices of continual tracking and monitoring through the year groups. Progress measures are grounded in the reliability of prediction; they point to the hype and expectations that Big Data will render the future knowable and manageable (Eynon 2013; Kitchin 2014). An irreverent twitter feed is devoted to the attractive graphs produced by schools showing coloured trajectories of students, described as the 'Big Gallery of Data Nonsense'.

Similar over-reliance on producing progress data even when it is meaningless was evident in this quote from the Grouping Project:

> 'The other thing we started doing because of the fear of Ofsted, because we're due one soon and we're worried about going back into required improvement, is we've started doing [pupil progress meetings]. We do three pupil progress meetings a year, then we do three midpoint ones in between each of them, where we go back and we reassess any child that wasn't at the right point and any child who is on the Pupil Premium list. We reassessed them so their data has to go up in between. Then when you come to the pupil progress meeting, it has to have gone up again. The idea almost being that *you can double their rate of progress by meeting more often.*' (Teacher, Focus Group 2)

For this teacher, the system of producing data to show progress has become an alternative reality, detached from the children in her class, providing further evidence of the distancing described earlier, and the reduction of the child to numbers. Those not making enough progress (and those on Pupil Premium, which indicates eligibility for FSM) are simply reassessed to make them 'go up', and then go up again. Of course, assessing children again or having more meetings does not make children make progress, but in this case the pressure exerted by the meetings seems to have the effect of nudging the teacher to reassess and ensure everyone makes progress, whatever the reality. This is an alternative strategy to the interventions discussed earlier, which deals with the problems produced by the data, where they fail to tell the right story. One way or another, as one teacher in a previous study commented, 'nobody's allowed to fall behind' (Roberts-Holmes and Bradbury 2016, p. 604).

But, however much we might manipulate the data, some children do reach the end of primary or secondary school not reaching 'expected levels', and progress measures are another tool to define those seen as failing. Importantly, systems based on *expected progress*, as defined through Progress 8 for example, also provide another means of division between pupils, into those fitting the trajectory, and those failing to make enough progress. To use the language heard in schools, some children's 'flight path' is below the expected route, raising the spectre of 'slower' learner labels. This resonates with the 'slower progress of development' discourse seen in early years (Bradbury 2013b). Progress data become another technology which defines some pupils as inadequate or 'lower ability' when they do not fit the pattern of 'normal' progress, all while appearing to be sensitive to the different intakes of schools and their efforts in moving every child on. Schools, as 'sorting and ranking institutions' (Ladwig and McPherson 2017, p. 355) use the language of progress to re-inscribe divisions between the norm and other, where the norm is expected progress.

## The ability spectrum and inequality

I turn now to the relationship between data and inequality. The accountability regime based on statutory assessment has been shown repeatedly to reproduce disparities by class, race and gender though assessment systems (Gillborn and Youdell 2000; Bradbury 2013b; Gillborn et al 2017). This regime underlies the process of datafication and should not be ignored as a structuring framework for what happens in schools, as mentioned. Data form the basis for practices which establish and maintain the idea of fixed ability, especially grouping systems:

> Datafication has certainly weakened the argumentative powers of actors committed to the comprehensive ideal and concerned about the inequitable outcomes of ability grouping in neoliberal policy settings ... the professional and education policy debate has depoliticised and marginalized communitarian thinking in relation to schooling. (Neumann 2021, p. 18)

The prominence of data has an impact on the frames of the debate about equality in education, narrowing what it is possible to argue – because no one can argue with the numbers – and pushing other conceptions of learning to the margins. The day-to-day mundane realities of datafication, such as the production of spreadsheets of attainment data and the filling of pupil tracking data, also have a role in perpetuating inequality through their mutually reinforcing relationship with concepts of ability.

The starting point of the argument about data and inequality is that datafication operates on the basis of definitions – of normal, expected, acceptable – which are linked to numbers and ranges of numbers. This creation of a framework of standards constructs the production of data as an objective and standardised process; we assess you all on the same things, so that must be fair (and of course, this means that these things matter). Numbers are produced, laid down in various forms, and re-translated into graphs and charts and trajectories of progress. This is a world where some boxes on the excel spreadsheet are red, and others are green. There is no broader consideration of the social factors at play – because this allocation is done by a computer, based on the input values determined at the start. Rules are applied equally to all in what could be described as a colour-blind or more accurately child-blind system. Yet the norm still has huge power, despite the proliferation of data which make it less obvious, as the numbers take on new forms and consequences.

Power operates through the norm, encased in the data, in disciplinary ways – ability groups, rankings, selective systems for grammar schools make real-life differences to children's lives. It also works to exclude some completely – for example in the use of an alternative assessment scale (the P scale) used for SEND children in primary education. The norm means that others must be worked on through interventions; this is a powerful application of the norm to identify the target of resources to restore normality.

Data are used to label children as high or low ability, providing the numerical authority for these labels. They also provide evidence of the idea that ability is something which we have in varying amounts, on a spectrum. Data are linked to inherent characteristics, so that it appears that 'ranking represents what is "naturally" internal and fixed to those bodies' (Ladwig and McPherson 2017, p. 365) – though of course, the numbers may not have always been seen as evidence of some innate quality. Databases on student attainment suggest that data is *precise* and *accurate*, providing the 'pseudo-security of numbers' (Biesta 2017, p. 317), whereas the reality experienced by many teachers is far more 'messy'. As Stobart comments, 'We can measure, and generate scores and ratings, for just about anything ... The critical step is what we infer from these' (2008, p. 34). Seeing a graph of a normal distribution, for example, makes common-sense the idea that there will be some higher or lower achievers, but most will be in the middle. It does not allow for questions about what is being assessed and on what basis, instead simply re-inscribing a discourse of differential attainment as inevitable.

This myth of neutrality is vital in reproducing inequalities in education. Let us consider first the disparities in attainment by ethnicity, as reported by the government (UK Government 2020a, 2020b). Year after year, the data provide the narrative that children from particular ethnic groups are more likely to gain the expected levels at GCSE or in Key Stage 2 SATs, and others are less likely. As Gillborn et al have established, whatever the measure, Black students have been one and a half times less likely to achieve the expected standard at GCSE than white students for the last 25 years (2017). This narrative feeds into low expectations for some and the concomitant higher expectations for the groups who are consistently higher attaining (and thus labelled a 'model minority', in some cases). The cycle is self-perpetuating (Bradbury 2013b): data provides evidence of difference; different expectation reproduce the data. Yet the system is seen as neutral and objective, despite consistent evidence that school practices such as grouping, tiered exam papers, lower expectations and teacher assessments, and educational triage disadvantage students from some ethnic groups and those on FSM (Gillborn and Youdell 2000; Gillborn 2013; Bradbury 2013b; Campbell 2014; Archer et al 2018).

Moreover, on an individual level, the recording of data solidifies identities, constituting the child as having a fixed amount of intelligence or merit. It ignores the differences between children from one day to the next based on their mood and external influences: you simply are a Grade 5 student, or a 'greater depth' pupil in Year 6, because the data tell us so. The pinnacle of this reductionism can be seen in the attempt to use teacher observations regarding everything from listening skills to toilet training to number recognition to produce a single score for each child on entry to school through Baseline Assessment, in a dramatic distillation of vast complexity into one number. In this world, the child is the data and the data are the child; be they high ability or low. This level of fixity raises real concerns about the reproduction of stereotypes about racial differences in intelligence, such as the 'Chinese geek' discourse (Archer and Francis 2007). These stereotypes circumscribe who can occupy positions of high-ability status with intelligibility, and thus there is a danger that once labelled, some children are unable to alter their line of flight through school, while the data make this flight path seem like good progress. In the case of Baseline Assessment in its 2015 iteration, this was a particular problem with children who spoke English as an additional language as they were unable in some cases to respond to the test at all, and were therefore given low scores which set up low expectations. As a headteacher I interviewed at the time commented:

> 'You know you don't want limiting judgements at this point. Because obviously what you are looking to do is open potential up, and I know that sometimes by measuring that and saying you could have issues here it might enable you to do that, but actually it can lead to low expectations as well. So obviously what we are in the business of trying to do is identify the needs as early as possible, but what you are not wanting to do is to say this is happening here, therefore this is what we expect of you here; that might be too low.' (Head, Cedar)

As we see in CRT scholarship, neutral systems set in place by assessment are often anything but neutral; they have real effects on judgements and expectations (Gillborn et al 2018).

For some, there are inevitable links between the testing regime as a differentiating exercise and the history of racialised intelligence levels: Lowe (1997) 'sees a clear eugenicist strand in the contemporary obsession with testing so as to identify different "ability levels" suitable for differential treatment' (cited in Gillborn 2010, p. 244). While the current school system, in the main,[3] does not allocate children to different schools based on testing, as in the era of the tripartite system, we can see the enactment of these ideas in schools' practices of setting and streaming, and the provision of different programmes of study at GCSE (Archer et al 2018). These are practices, as discussed in Chapter 3, with raced and classed effects, inextricably linked with damaging eugenic ideas based on deterministic assumptions and a belief in the accuracy of measuring 'ability'.

Some research data from the Grouping Project illustrates this solidifying process, where data and ability discourses work together to make differences appear neutrally produced. Again, the focus is largely on class and children receiving FSM, as this is what emerged from the data. Throughout the project, the issue of group allocation being related to children's backgrounds was noted as a concern by many participants; one survey respondent explained "I think we end up with middle class and not middle class groups" (W). This reflects the intelligibility of middle-class children as 'higher ability', as also evidenced by comments which suggested middle-class parents would complain if their child were not 'correctly' allocated to the higher groups.

In contrast, children for whom the school receives Pupil Premium funding were linked with lower attainment levels and therefore subject to intervention:

> 'Yes, so the majority of the Pupil Premium are with me who are just one step behind where they should be. But then our Pupil Premium children don't do any reading at home, none. So then we have a TA, a teaching assistant, her job is just to read with the Pupil Premium children and to try to catch them up.' (School Leader, Whiteread Primary)

These children's home lives are seen as the justification for their placement 'one step behind'; their data combine with their social class to make additional support necessary. Here we see how practice, data and class-based assumptions combine to position these children as 'behind' the norm.

## The shift on from data?

As mentioned early in this chapter, the pressures of this data obsession in terms of workload have led to calls for reform. The Teacher Workload Advisory Group concluded: 'In a number of schools, there are data practices that are not helpful for pupil progress and that increase teacher workload. Schools should question their existing practice to change this' (Teacher Workload Advisory Group 2018, p. 5). In response, the then Secretary of State for Education, Damien Hinds, wrote to local authorities and Academy Trust leaders explaining that 'we want to make sure that schools are only collecting the data they need, and not collecting or monitoring unnecessary data for audit purposes' (Damien Hinds 2019, p. 1). Changes to the framework for inspection by Ofsted included reforms designed to discourage schools from collecting data specifically for inspection. Hinds explained, 'Inspectors will not look at non-statutory internal progress and attainment data' (2019, p. 2). However, the statutory data collected, in primary schools at least, are vast: there are statutory assessments in Reception and Years 1, 2, 4 and 6 (all but two years of primary school), and there is scepticism over the idea that Ofsted will not be looking at data under the new framework for inspection. Similarly, secondary schools rely on their regular internal assessments to monitor 'value added' in relation to their Progress 8 scores. It is also important to bear in mind that schools may find the data useful, as Hardy's study of an Australian secondary school's use of data concludes:

> the numbers were always and everywhere pervasive and substantive in their effects, and in sometimes deeply troubling ways, they also served to stimulate inquiry and learning that was sometimes clearly valuable and, sometimes substantive, and enabled teachers to engage with their students' work and learning in often-productive ways. (Hardy 2021, p. 60)

It seems unlikely that schools will feel confident to dismantle their data infrastructures yet.

The loss of statutory assessments in 2020 due to the COVID-19 pandemic raised further questions about the role and importance of data. With schools closed through the spring and summer, it was announced that all exams in secondary schools (GCSEs and A levels) and statutory assessments in primary schools (EYFS Profile, SATs in Key Stage 1 and 2, the PSC and the Multiplication Tables Check) were to be abandoned. Suddenly, the end result of many years of assessing pupils disappeared; for primary schools, the culmination of many years of hard work was simply gone. Given the pressure and anxiety caused by SATs, and the organisation often of the whole school around improving results (Bradbury 2019d), this was a real shock to the system. Exam grades in secondary school were replaced with teacher assessments based on predicted grades, with great significance for students applying for university and progressing onto post-16 courses. However, results created by teachers will never have the same significance as exam results as they are subject to teacher biases; accusations of over-grading began before the publication of grades (Lough 2020a). This will be an issue again in 2021 with the cancellation of SATs and A level and GCSE exams.

What this use of teacher assessment does reveal, however, is the continued belief in pupils having a set ability, which can be reflected by data. Explanations of the use of teacher assessments were based on the idea that teachers *know* their pupils; it suggests that pupils are attaining at a set and measurable grade, whether we apply the test to them or not. This is significant because, as I have argued in relation to much younger pupils, teacher 'knowledge' is not neutral (Bradbury 2013b). Assessments by teachers frequently reproduce the disparities in attainment by race and class we see in exam results, and may in fact exacerbate these differences (Murphy and Wyness 2020). Concerns have been expressed at the potential for predicted grades to reproduce these disparities (Akpan 2020). It remains to be seen how this new method of producing data disrupts the datafication process, if at all. I return to the possibilities for this shift in thinking about data in the concluding chapter.

## Conclusion

This chapter has provided an overview of a second educational development, summarised as datafication, and how it relates to concepts of ability and inequality. Despite the hope of reducing inequalities through access to technology (Macgilchrist 2019), the evidence presented here suggests that in education the increased use of data facilitated by advances in technology has the effect of *reproducing* inequalities. The links between data and ability grouping, the solidity of numerical labels, and underlying pressures of producing data within a high-stakes accountability system are all contributors to the consistent disparities in education by class and race. In Foucauldian terms, data are disciplinary, classifying students against set norms, but also regulatory in their application to whole populations (as we saw in Chapter 2's attainment data). They are used at both levels to sort, label and manage individuals and the whole student body, largely through the application of norms.

Recent developments such as the attempt to reduce reliance on data from government and the loss of assessments in 2020 due to the pandemic have some potential to disrupt this connection between data, ability and the production of inequality, but they also have the potential to exacerbate this problem.

One point I wish to emphasise here is the co-reliance of data and ability as discursive formations. Different abilities produce different data, and data 'prove' different abilities. Returning to the descriptions of 'ability' discussed in Chapter 2, we can see the strength of the idea that children can be placed in order on a spectrum; they simply are low or high, because the data tell us so. Ability is "Where a child is" or "A sliding scale where peers are compared to each other, with the highest achievers at the top and SEND learners at the bottom" (W); alternatively ability is exactly the same as 'assessment scores', or a position in relation to the norm – "Whether they are working at age related expectations, higher or below". These ideas of ability as positional are based, like datafication, on a principle of objective measurement as the best means to understand the child as learner. These ideas are established through discourses of *standardisation* (we all agree what 'age related' means) 'as a prerequisite to objectivity'; this is not inevitable, indeed 'objectivity-making' takes hard work (Williamson and Piattoeva 2019, pp. 65, after Jasanoff 2011). This construction of objectivity means that when thinking about ability we do not take into account either the socially contingent nature of all forms of measurement, or the wider social context in which these hierarchies are constructed. The principle of measurable ability undergirds a mythical meritocratic view of society where each child has an equal chance to achieve high scores or 'good progress', and their success in doing so is easily assessed.

In the following concluding chapter, I consider how the different concepts of ability revived by neuroscience and datafication operate together, and who gains from contemporary myths of meritocracy. I then turn to the possibilities for thinking differently, and the potential for disruption provided by the post-pandemic context.

# 6

# Challenging ability, inequality and the myth of meritocracy in the post-pandemic era

## Introduction

This book has sought to examine in detail how discourses of 'ability' as fixed and measurable, embedded within broader discourses of meritocracy, reproduce inequalities in education. I have argued that ability as discourse is a set of parameters which define and maintain acceptable truths within schooling, which can have pernicious effects. Two developments in education, related to data and to neuroscience, were used to consider how ability discourses operate at this historical juncture – within the current *episteme* – in a neoliberal education system shaped by a decade of Conservative-led governments. The aim was to uncover the choices that are made about how we understand children's 'ability' through scrutiny of the impact of new developments. This endeavour was informed by theoretical perspectives from Foucault on discipline and regulation, and influenced by CRT, which asks questions about how everyday workings of systems can disadvantage minoritised groups.

During the period of writing of this book, the emergence of a new coronavirus and the resulting pandemic brought dramatic shifts in terms of education, but also society and the economy. These continue as the crisis unfolds and there is increasingly awareness of the long-term impacts of COVID-19. One of these impacts is a greater focus on educational inequality, as the idea that attainment gaps would be increased by children learning at home became a familiar topic in the media. It will take many years for the effects of these events to be understood, but we can begin to explore what the post-pandemic era might look like in education, and how it can be reshaped in equitable ways, particularly as research on the first wave of the pandemic is published.

As I write, the UK is experiencing a crisis which has presented problems for education unlike any previously seen: how to teach children when they cannot be physically together? How to ensure children's different experiences when learning at home do not reproduce or exacerbate the social inequalities which have been a hallmark of the education system for decades? How to use technology to support children, without further disadvantaging those on the wrong side of the 'digital divide'? And how to fairly assess children whose learning has been disrupted over a long period?

These questions are evolving as the conversation shifts to the long-term impact, and to what needs to be done in the immediate future to alleviate the impact of the pandemic. These new questions involve such thorny issues as how to teach children when they are socially distanced and unable to move groups; how to assess students fairly when they have had such different experiences at home; and significantly, how to support children who may have experienced bereavement, ill-health or serious financial difficulty during the pandemic. The prominence of issues such as the provision of free school meals for pupils over the school holidays (BBC News 2020) has highlighted how essential schools have become in providing the most basic of human needs – food. Research undertaken with my UCL Institute of Education colleagues has revealed the extent of schools' roles in providing free meals and other welfare-related services during the first lockdown period of spring 2020 (Bradbury et al 2020; Moss et al 2020; Wyse et al 2020). The engagement of the wider public and politicians with the long-standing but currently severe issue of child poverty is an important outcome of the pandemic, raising questions about the policies of austerity and schools' ability to replace the welfare state (Monroe 2020; Moss 2020a). The crisis has revealed the 'seismic fault line' in the system, showing that 'schooling in disadvantaged areas has become a branch of social services, propping up and supporting a much depleted and under-resourced welfare state' (Reay 2020a, p. 312). We also know that more teachers were concerned about the impact on learning of the first lockdown in schools serving disadvantaged areas (ILC 2020b); though the literature suggests that estimates of 'learning loss' in this unprecedented situation are difficult to predict (Harmey and Moss 2020).

By the time this book is published, we may know a little more about the impact of COVID-19 and how successful the immediate attempts were to reduce the negative effects of the disease, but the longer-term consequences of the pandemic will be revealed over the coming years, as narratives about what was done well or done badly begin to settle.

The dramatic impact of the pandemic on education, on teachers, parents and children, has another consequence: the opportunity to rebuild, or recover, in ways which are different, so that we move towards a more ethical, equal post-pandemic education system. I want to use this last chapter to consider what that system might look like, alongside reviewing the arguments made thus far. This concluding chapter includes discussions of the tensions and commonalities between the two developments of datafication and increased use of neuroscience, the overlaying of multiple conceptions of ability, and the effect of this confusion – both in the 2010s and into the post-COVID future. I also explain more specifically who the winners are in this supposedly meritocratic game, and how the power of those who are successful is a major barrier to thinking differently. I begin with a return to the two developments which were the focus of Chapters 4 and 5.

## Brains and data: tensions and commonalities

While I have considered these two developments separately in previous chapters, there are clearly some points of commonality and some tensions between them which require further exploration. Both trends are rhetorically positioned in education as part of an enlightenment-style narrative of progress through science, where new technology allows us to understand learning in more accurate and complex ways. They are the latest episodes in a story we tell ourselves about how much better things are now than they were in the past, and how modern we are. Now, in a time of crisis, they offer hope and resolution: we can teach and assess children online and measure their success through apps! We can use what we know about traumatised brains to support children to recover!

There are also areas where neuroscience and data (or more broadly computational developments) overlap, in both practical and theoretical terms. In some developing areas of educational technology, the brain is being used to provide inspiration for artificial intelligence systems in education, which in turn have an effect on the human brains using them (Williamson et al 2018). These neurocomputational developments produce new 'brain-computer-society entanglements' (Ienca and Andorno 2017 p. 5, cited in Williamson et al 2018, p. 262); they represent 'a kind of biosocial enthusiasm about the plasticity of the brain and epigenetic modulation' (2018, p. 272) which results in different conceptions of the learner. While this development is still in its infancy, it reminds us of the need for critique of the relations between science, technology and social relations, particularly in fields where there are attempts to 'rewire plastic brains to fit particular commercial and governmental aspirations' (2018, p. 273). There is also a convergence in the use of data infrastructures to support the advancement of education policy on SEL, which is based on insights from psychology and economics (Williamson 2019).

More theoretically, we can see the importance of the norm, in both developments, and the designation of those 'above' and 'below' expectations. The norm operates powerfully within each development to create certainty and distinction, whether this be between the damaged infant brain and the normal one, or between those 'at expected levels' and those at 'greater depth'. Furthermore, both are based on a 'construction of objectivity' (Williamson and Piattoeva 2019); a culture which treats numbers and science as neutral, rather than socially constructed; based on fact, rather than part of networks of power. As discussed, the visual image of the brain scan carries great legitimising weight: scans 'constitute personhood in neurological terms' (Millei and Joronen 2016, p. 400), allowing broader emotional and social conclusions to be drawn from purely neurological information.

Significantly, there are areas where data and the influence of science more broadly coalesce in ways which reproduce inequality. Epigenetics, in particular, appears to justify the kind of hereditarian claims of past eugenics; there is in operation 'a new eugenics whereby black students are systematically disadvantaged but blamed for their own failure by assessments that lend racist stereotypes a spurious air of scientific respectability' (Gillborn 2010, p. 231). This 'new geneism' revives hereditarian notions of genetically fixed intelligence which vary by racial group, while the accountability system provides further data as evidence of racial difference. From a CRT perspective, scientific revelations and the growth of data combine here in a dangerous new tool for the dismissal of minoritised success and the promotion of white interests (Gillborn 2016). I would argue that the risk of 'ideology masquerading as science' (Rose 2009, p. 788, cited in Gillborn 2016, p. 383) is increased during this period of the COVID-19 emergency, when the world has become so reliant on scientists' advice. Together data and neuroscience provide authority and legitimacy, through recourse to science and numbers, to ideas about fundamental group differences – on the basis of race but also class – which many thought were long discredited. The prominence of Dominic Cummings, the prime minister's key adviser, during the COVID-19 crisis, despite his publicly criticised views on eugenic themes (Mason and Sample 2020), shows this shift in views of what is acceptable. Similarly, the publication of books such as Nicholas Wade's *A Troublesome Inheritance* (see Murray 2014) suggests that there is still money to be made in such controversial views, when they make claims to new 'insights'. As Gillborn has stated, 'the colourblind façade repackages centuries old stereotypes in shiny new DNA-patterned bundles' (2016, p. 382). The 'new knowledge' of neuroscience combined with the technology-driven production of data is a powerful force driving our view of children as measurable and knowable, and thus we can justifiably use labels such as 'damaged' or 'behind' with confidence and authority. I am reminded of Ball's statement about power as productive – 'a lot of the time it "makes us up" rather than grinds us down' (Ball 2013, p. 31).

However, there are also areas of tension between these two developments, as I am sure readers will have recognised through the preceding chapters. I have argued that neuroscience and data can be seen as undergirding two different views of ability – ability as innate, and as measurable and fixed respectively – which the research data from the Grouping in Early Years and Key Stage 1 project revealed were prominent in teachers' conceptions of the term. There are clearly tensions between these two views, which play out in how neuroscience and data are operationalised in education, and in turn are affected by new scientific developments such as epigenetics. I explore these tensions in the following section.

## Multiple conceptions of ability: confusion and certainty

One of the themes of this book has been the confusion and slipperiness of the term ability, and the way in which discourses of fixedness and the influence of the environment sometimes operate together in contradictory ways. We have seen how discourses which associate the quality of the home learning environment with educational success sit alongside a view of children as inherently 'bright', for instance. Underlying these parallel conceptions of how intelligence operates are two scientific theories, of 'hard' heritability, innateness, fixed intelligence; and of 'soft' heritability, epigenetics and the influence of the environment (including parenting and education) on how genes operate. Ball has argued that the combination of truth and power 'represented in particular in sciences of intelligence … remain as the foundations to education in the present' (Ball 2013, p. 64); thus is it perhaps logical that the divergence of newer science from the *genes=destiny* equation has allowed for a proliferation of conceptions of intelligence, which we can see in teachers' descriptions. Perhaps we are all, to put it simply, confused about what these new ideas mean for how we understand intelligence, and reluctant to shift from the idea of people as hard-wired to be clever or not. As discussed in Chapter 2, some genetic work has been used to support notions of fixed ability, and despite concerns about a new determinism, scholars such as Plomin have found new audiences for their argument that genes influence attainment (Dorling and Tomlinson 2016). At the same time as these developments have gained traction in public discourse, the obsession of an accountability-based high-stakes testing system with data and tracking revives the older less fashionable notion of fixed and measurable ability and the practices of classification into high/middle/low or into ability groups or sets. These different views, illogically, seem to sit comfortably together in some teachers' descriptions. That this is illogical is irrelevant, however, when thinking about the impact of these views.

But why should the newer version of intelligence, as fixed to a certain extent by genes but influenced by environment, not replace the old version? Dorling and Tomlinson discuss this 'resurfacing' of eugenic notions of inherited ability, noting that 'policy-makers have persisted in their beliefs about the inferior "intelligence" of social class and racial groups, using genetic arguments about ability and potential which supposedly lead to differential educational attainment' (Dorling and Tomlinson 2016, p. 58). They argue, using international comparisons of attainment levels and measures of inequality in incomes, that ideas about intelligence are more prominent in societies with greater levels of inequality and lower educational outcomes: 'It is not accidental that the less successful countries in basic education, the USA and UK, which are also the most economically unequal, have reverted to hereditarian and pseudo-eugenic explanations for educational performance, which appears to be influencing political elite thinking' (Dorling and Tomlinson 2016, p. 70).

Scientific ideas about inherent variation in capability are being revived and used in order to justify inequalities in society. As Meloni argues, throughout history biological ideas have been linked to political arguments; these produce 'the specific alignment of science and values we have assumed natural or logical' (Meloni 2016, p. 131, cited in Youdell 2016, p. 972). It is this reason, perhaps, that allows both the ideas of fixedness and the influence of environment to flourish: both explain and allow for the maintenance of raced and classed inequalities. The confusion and contradiction do not matter, if we see these two explanations as serving the same purpose. To examine this further, I now turn to a consideration of who succeeds in this mythical meritocracy.

## The winners in the game of 'meritocracy' and the barriers to change

So where does this leave us in terms of schooling and the meritocratic ideal? Learning from CRT, our starting point should be to ask who gains and who suffers, and who has the power to change this state of affairs. In other words, what does the discourse of ability, whether it be innate or measurable or both, *do* within the education system, and why do such inequalities result? After all, as I discussed in Chapter 3, disparities in education in terms of race and class have been long-standing features of the education system in England.

Overall, my argument is that the middle-class, white and English-speaking child gains through current discourses of 'ability', though this may be indirectly, and of course the gain is not felt uniformly or by every child without exception. There are other groups of pupils who succeed too, such as children from the Indian and Chinese communities, but, as I and others have argued elsewhere, this may not be positioned as 'authentic' success (Archer 2008; Bradbury 2013a). However, in broad terms, we see how class and ethnic group intersect to create a positionality which is more likely to be regarded as 'high ability'. At the start of this book I mentioned my ambiguous feelings about watching my own (white and middle-class) daughters enter the school system in the knowledge that they will benefit from these discourses, to an even greater extent than I did. I see my eldest daughter being placed in the 'top group' for phonics, and my middle daughter being encouraged to learn to read in nursery in special one-to-one sessions with the teacher; they are made more confident and pushed harder because they are labelled as 'bright'. I recognise the experience from my own schooling; although they cannot see it, something is happening to my daughters which will have a very positive impact on their lives. As Reay argues, the 'misrecognition of educational advantage that meritocracy authorises allows the economic, social, and cultural capitals that define educational success to be read as inherent ability' (2020, p. 408). What it is important to remember, is that this cannot occur without the concomitant labelling of other children as 'low ability', or 'behind'. Having winners means having losers, and it is those children from poorer and minoritised backgrounds who suffer in this game of 'ability'.

The myth that everyone has an equal chance is powerful, and of course attractive both to those who gain and to those for whom it offers hope. When my daughter is labelled as achieving 'greater depth', I cannot help but feel pleased; ability has real rewards for those who are labelled 'high ability', material and symbolic. It is a hard task to dismantle a system and thus wrestle those rewards from those who already hold the most power:

> The old myth about the ability and variability of potential
> in children is a comforting myth for those who are uneasy

> with the degree of inequality they seek and would rather seek to justify it than confront it. The myth of inherent potential helps some explain to themselves why they are privileged. (Dorling and Tomlinson 2016, p. 56)

One of the major barriers to thinking differently about ability is then that it would make the privilege of many in society more visible. It is far easier to argue that we can all succeed, and we all have a chance, and some of us have simply worked harder and were born more intelligent, than to see society as having prejudice and inequality embedded firmly within it. As Reay argues, 'The very notion of merit undercuts any idea of radical change as an alternative to neoliberal capitalism, instead generating policy options that work within existing structures rather than challenging them' (2020, p. 61); it is difficult to think differently when the idea of merit is so embedded within our politics. She cites research by Gaffney and Baumberg which shows that the UK has high levels of belief in meritocracy but also low levels of social mobility, compared to other comparable countries (2020, p. 406); this 'fantasy' hides the reproductive element of the education system. Thus, meritocracy is 'the flimsy sticking plaster patching up a "rotten public realm"' (2020, p. 406).

Furthermore, a major barrier is the fact that the discourse of ability and its associated practices such as grouping and setting are ingrained within the education system, and have been for decades (White 2006; Francis et al 2017). Many of the teachers in the Grouping Project accepted this term as indicating an innate and determined level of intelligence – both in the survey and the interviews. Importantly, many of the teachers questioned or challenged the practice of grouping by ability, but often there was very little time or space for alternative ways of organising their classroom, or the school structures were too well established to suggest a different system. Grouping was described as a 'necessary evil' within the current context (Bradbury and Roberts-Holmes 2017b). Even fewer of the respondents, however, actually questioned the underlying concept of ability; for most, the issue with grouping was making the differences between children visible to them, rather than the problem of ordering children by ability in general (Bradbury 2019e). Thus the objection was to the revealing of ability levels, rather than the levels themselves. There were also real pressures to prepare for assessments and in some cases school policies on grouping, which drove teachers' practice, even when they did not agree with grouping; this was indicative of a culture of 'doing without believing' in teaching, found more widely (Braun and Maguire 2020). The two teachers within the study who had been able to change their practice based on their objection to the concept of ability both had a specific reason for doing so, justified by an external reasoning. One was a senior leader in his school who had undertaken a dedicated exploration of the impact of grouping, and changed school policy as a result, and the other was a newer teacher who used her masters' dissertation to get approval from the headteacher to try out mixed groups (see Bradbury 2019e for more detail). These exceptional examples show the difficulty in questioning ingrained assumptions, at the same time as offering hope that where there is time and space to think differently, shifts in views of ability can results in changes to practice and thus have an impact on children.

There is also great potential, within the current COVID-19 context, for shifts that were introduced as temporary measures to become embedded within education, in ways which will preserve the status quo. Williamson et al talk of 'the context of changes currently being experienced at planetary scale, and potentially dramatic shifts in the relationships between science, technology and society' (2020b, p. 107). The increased use of digital methods of teaching during lockdown can sound ominously like a smokescreen for increased dataveillance and further commercial encroachment into state education, as they comment: 'efforts to datafy the student experience of education during the pandemic need to be understood as an extreme manifestation of longer-term aspirations to render education legible as numbers through increasingly pervasive technologies and techniques of surveillance' (Williamson et al 2020b, p. 113). In this manifestation, the pandemic is the catalyst for the further datafication of education. Like the policy 'ratchet' (Ball 2008), once teachers and students have experienced online learning, they cannot go back, instead seeing face-to-face teaching as inefficient. This is relevant here because these technologies are part of the aspiration to 'render education legible as numbers', and in turn render children machine readable, as data points. Teachers can see who is online, and pupils' level of interaction with the material set, as well as scoring and marking work. The interaction between teacher and pupils becomes digital rather than interpersonal, as they send documents back and forth, or talk via messaging. Schools and parents, now familiar with digital learning platforms, have continued to use these even when children are back at school.

Similarly, the increased focus on health more widely, and the mental health of children during lockdown in particular, provide scope for a further focus on the brain in education. The concerns about vulnerable children's experiences during their time at home, and the well-established discourse that poorer children were doing fewer hours of schoolwork than their more affluent peers (EEF 2020), reprise the discourses around less conducive HLEs and trauma-affected brains discussed in Chapter 4. Indeed, the NEU provided a course titled 'COVID19: Understanding and dealing with the traumatic effects of the pandemic on your students', run partly by Trauma Informed Schools, in July 2020 (NEU 2020). This suggests that there is potential for the dangerous elisions of poverty and damaged brains to continue. This – and other ideas – come from a well-meaning place of concern for children's welfare, but they simultaneously propagate and reinforce the reduction of children to their brains, and the associations between background and attainment. In a time when these associations are already a common trope in the media, this is a real concern.

## The future of 'ability': post-pandemic hope

As examined earlier, there are significant barriers to changing how people think and talk about ability in schools, particularly its ingrained nature from policy to the classroom, and its relationship to the idea of meritocracy, which is both politically and personally attractive to many of those who wield the most power. It is important to emphasise here that ability as a discourse functions as a *regime of truth*, in Foucauldian terms, which has both disciplinary and regulatory functions – operating on the individual and the population: 'teachers' practices, and those of their pupils too, are seen as being governed by discourses of schooling which define what is (in)appropriate, (un)acceptable and (ab)normal – literally, how life should be ordered' (Pratt and Alderton 2019, p. 585).

Ability has disciplinary functions in the classroom; it is a key part of the micropractices of power (Gore 1995) that dominate school practices – *classification, distribution, normalisation*. These practices, and grouping in particular, have real effects on children in terms of confidence and their view of themselves as learners (Hargreaves et al 2021; Francis et al 2020). But it also has a function in the 'ordering of life' at the level of the population: the idea that ability is fixed and measurable facilitates systems of schooling in which pupils take different paths, for example – to do otherwise would be inefficient. Meritocracy, as conceived of by the politicians who talk of allowing children to go 'as far as their talents take them', is a myth built on the idea that the best will rise up from the general populace, if given the chance. It is this operation at the levels of discipline *and* regulation which makes the discourse of ability very difficult to challenge.

Thinking differently is not easy: we are seduced by the 'banality of numbers' (Ball 2018), the chance to represent a child's success or failure with some fixity, rather than accept the complexity of the reality. We believe in the power of the brain and the scientists who purport to make this mystery knowable and understandable. But, in this phase of reconnection, recovery and rebuilding (Moss 2020b), after a global health emergency which has altered everyday life, destroyed economies and damaged politicians' reputations, there is perhaps a new space to think about schooling differently. There is a chance, even if it is a small one, to rebuild with different principles; as one commentator put it, referring to the goodwill towards teachers, 'We mustn't waste the opportunity COVID-19 has given us' (Mroz 2020). Research on teachers' views has similarly found a strong desire to 'build back better' (Moss et al 2020); there is potential for change in a number of areas related to ability and inequality.

First of all, there is the potential to ask questions about statutory testing, given the abandonment of all tests and exams in 2020. This decision meant that there was no need for the Year 6 curriculum to be dominated by the SATs subjects of English and maths, as previously (Bradbury 2019d). Year 1 teachers did not need to coach their children in how to pass the PSC, and Year 4 did not focus on times tables in preparation for the Multiplication Tables Check. Secondary teachers did not need to spend time preparing their students for exams, with lessons on revision technique and writing in exam conditions (Gewirtz et al 2019). The narrowing of the curriculum due to statutory testing was absent, providing an opportunity for teachers to see how different their priorities could be. This unusual experiment in *not* testing, for the first time in decades, has expanded the parameters of what is possible. Furthermore, the lack of external tests has perhaps allowed teachers time to reflect on the wider purposes of education; after all it is well established that

> working to any externally imposed set of measures with high-stakes consequences squeezes out the time, energy and 'head-space' teachers need if they are to be able to meaningfully engage in critical reflection and debate and make independent judgements that are grounded in and properly responsive to their in-depth first-hand knowledge of their students and the contexts in which they are working. (Gewirtz et al 2019, p. 19)

This responsiveness to students will be even more necessary – and hopefully possible – in the post-pandemic era. It may be simply irrelevant to conduct statutory tests which will be so affected by the pandemic; there may need to be different ways of holding schools to account, not simply based on how well they have conducted 'catch up' programmes (ILC 2020a; Lough 2020b). This disruption to the systematic allocation of children to numbers and grades for at least one year has the potential to also disrupt the discourse of children as 'able' on a spectrum, which was so strong in teachers' discussions of the term pre-pandemic. Labels such as 'at age related expectation' become meaningless if you are not testing against an expectation; instead, it is possible to think of the child's learning in broader terms.

This new space to think differently about assessment is evident in campaigns for the government to abandon SATs tests and other statutory assessment in 2021, given the disruption to learning (ILC, 2020a; More than a Score 2020). In October 2020 a letter in *The Times* signed by hundreds of primary headteachers argued 'we cannot afford to waste any more face-to-face teaching time on statutory tests that will cause undue anxiety' (Times 2020) and the headteachers' union passed a motion calling for the tests to be scrapped (Civinini 2020). In January 2021, as schools switched again to remote learning during the third lockdown in England, it was announced that SATs would be abandoned again (Whittaker, 2021).

At secondary level, the A level and GCSE fiasco of the summer of 2020, when teacher-assessed grades awarded by schools were 'corrected' by an algorithm until the government was forced to restore them, shook confidence in the exams and testing regime; as one commentator in the *TES* asked, 'Is it time to reboot our entire exams system?' (Tierney 2020). A new campaign group, Rethinking Assessment, was formed to start a conversation about how best to assess children in secondary. A key member, Peter Hyman, argues that the current system 'stifles the creativity of young people rather than liberating it. It causes unnecessary pressure rather than supporting the transition to adulthood' (Rethinking Assessment 2020). Their aim is to provide solutions to the problem of secondary assessment which will work in schools. A levels and GCSEs were also cancelled in 2021 due to disruption to schooling during the pandemic.

These new developments in the long-standing campaigns against high-stakes testing show how the pandemic has opened up new ways of thinking about established systems. If the current uncertainty about schools staying fully open continues into the longer term, alternative methods of assessing children in less time-specific ways will need to be considered: fewer exams, more ongoing assessment, lower-stakes assessments. The balance between assessment for accountability and assessment for learning will need to shift; while the latter remains a necessary part of schooling, the former distorts the curriculum (Bradbury 2019d). This is my post-pandemic hope, that we might see a system with less labelling of children in terms of numbers and grades, and in terms of ability; that there could be a move away from attempts to understand a child in these terms.

This links to a second possibility, which is that this is an opportunity to reframe learning as something affecting the whole child, dependent on their welfare. Evidence from the first lockdown suggests that schools were focused far more on the welfare of children, rather than their learning, during the pandemic (Bradbury 2020b; Moss et al 2020). One key point about learning has been brought to the fore in the pandemic – that children cannot learn if they are hungry, worried or stressed (Moss 2020a). As noted earlier, there is now space to think about the welfare role of schools, and their role within communities, and to value this aspect of education as much as assessment results. There is an opportunity to challenge the pressurised environment of schools and the pre-pandemic focus on testing and data, which had an impact on pupils' mental health (Gewirtz et al 2019). New 'recovery' curricula in the autumn of 2020 involved a focus on children's emotional strength and resilience, in recognition of the difficulties faced by pupils who have been out of school for months (Hayles 2020); these shifts in priorities could provoke longer-lasting changes in the curriculum, with less emphasis on measuring attainment in core subjects. There is also, I should add, a danger that the 'trauma-informed practice' discourse discussed in Chapter 4 is reinvigorated by this focus on children's welfare, as mentioned. But, if the simplifications of discourses which associate children from poorer families with 'damaged' brains can be avoided, I would argue there is potential for schools to justify a focus on children's welfare over results during the post-pandemic years.

Third, there is a chance to take the collectivity, empathy and care shown during the pandemic into the future; to focus on collaboration instead of competition. Schools have become central to many communities, providing food and support services (Bradbury 2020b); headteachers have relied upon their networks of colleagues for support (ILC 2020c). Schools might continue to work together as they recover from the pandemic, and reject the values of the market and league tables. Recommendations arising from research on the crisis have included a resetting of educational priorities, including 'more durable, more deliberative and more transparent ways of connecting all those involved in managing the many different aspects of education across a fragmented system' (ILC 2020c, p. 4). Much of this might be in response to a growing gulf between the teaching profession and the government through the crisis (Bradbury 2020a), but the collaborative efforts among schools have shown that alternative are possible.

That said, we must recognise that underlying many of the structures that might be changed, discussed earlier, there lies the powerful ideology of neoliberalism. This ideology justifies competition and demands statutory assessment for the purposes of accountability. It is embedded within the education sector at all levels, so that to think differently is a challenge for many teachers who have never worked in a different system (Wilkins 2011; Ball 2017). But even within this neoliberal framework, there is potential to assess schools differently – after all, neoliberalism is an ideology which evolves and adapts to survive (Peck and Tickell 2002; McGimpsey 2016). Schools could be held to account for the welfare of their pupils, if this could be assessed with nuance, in ways which do not fall back on numbers or grades, and this system operated without the pressures associated with Ofsted gradings. Success for a school could be conceived of more broadly, as about quality and depth of learning, well-being and cohesion, instead of simply understood as exam results and progress data. There were shifts in this direction before COVID, with the revised Ofsted framework of 2019, which committed to inspectors spending 'less time looking at exam results and test data, and more time considering how a [school] has achieved their results' (UK Government 2019b). This attempt to look more broadly at schools' achievements was welcomed by primary headteachers (Bradbury 2019d), though the framework was only in operation for a few months before the COVID-19 pandemic resulted in a pause on inspections. In July 2020 it was announced that inspections would resume in 2021, but Ofsted would conduct visits to schools during the autumn term of 2020. These visits would not result in official gradings, but 'outcomes of discussions' would be published (Speck 2020). According to the General Secretary of the NEU, attempts to assess how well schools have coped with the crisis 'may well be the most useful activity that Ofsted have undertaken in decades' (Bousted 2020, p. 441). During the third lockdown in early 2021, there continued to be discussion over the need for Ofsted inspection visits (Stewart 2021).

In the post-pandemic era, more significant steps to change the culture of short-term inspections, which only provide a snapshot of a school, are necessary to fundamentally disrupt the reliance on attainment data. Reform of the accountability system of statutory testing would also be required if schools were to be judged in more complex and nuanced ways, on children's welfare, depth and enjoyment of learning.

This would require significant political shifts, but ultimately these changes could provide conditions where discourses of ability could be less damaging.

## Conclusion

The main post-pandemic hope is of course some disruption to the fixed-ability thinking that has been the focus of this book. Like many others, I would argue that this is a necessary step in disrupting the practices which result from the idea that ability is fixed and measurable (Drummond and Yarker 2013). This notion of fixed ability, as Yarker argues, 'enables a host of fundamental questions about the purposes of education, as well as the practices of teaching, to be sidestepped' (2019, p. 3). It is only by questioning ability itself that we can begin to ask the wider questions which I have discussed earlier, about reforming the education system so that it works against inequality, rather than reproducing it.

The developments I have focused on here – datafication and neuroscience – are part of the current discourses of ability. They are not the only developments, of course, and as the pandemic continues to unfold, there may be new ways in which 'ability' discourses evolve. I would like to start a conversation about recognising ability for the constructed notion that it is, and the central role it plays in reproducing inequalities. This is a difficult conversation, but one which must be confronted if we wish to tackle the educational inequalities which are so prevalent in the education system.

# Notes

## Chapter 1

[1] I use 'race' here in quotation marks to emphasise the constructed nature of the term; however, for ease of reading the term is used without quotation marks from this point onwards. In line with CRT texts, I use the term 'minoritised' to describe non-White groups.

## Chapter 2

[1] Respondents to this survey were predominantly teachers in Key Stage 1 and Early Years, with some primary school leaders also taking part.

## Chapter 3

[1] I use the term inequalities here rather than discussing *equity*, as the former is in more popular use, but with an awareness that treating everyone equally does not result in equity.

[2] Data here are based on the figures from 2018 to 2019, as no statutory testing took place in 2020 due to the COVID-19 pandemic.

[3] Note that in these and the following data discussions, I have only included ethnic groups with more than 2000 pupils taking the assessment. This removes some groups such as Gypsy/Roma; this is not to dismiss the important discussions about attainment from these groups, but to allow for a clearer view of the overall picture. Indeed, there is extensive research on the attainment and experiences of these groups (see D'Arcy 2014; Myers et al 2010).

[4] The problems with using FSM as a proxy for class are well documented, particularly the confusion between being 'working class' and receiving FSM (Gillborn 2010). However, at this level of looking at the school population as a whole, the only available data are based on FSM.

[5] The highest temporary exclusion rates are for Traveller of Irish Heritage pupils at 17.42%, or 1,742 exclusions per 10,000 pupils and Gypsy and Roma pupils at 16.52%, or 1,652 per 10,000 pupils, but again, I have concentrated on the larger groups here. I have also left out the Unknown group here and in Table 3.2.

[6] The actual number of permanent exclusions in this year for Chinese pupils was three.

[7] Meloni also questions the idea that scientific racism has seen a simple resurgence due to genetic developments, instead arguing that there are multiple biologies which affect race in different ways – 'the struggle is not only over biology: it is also within biology' (Meloni 2017, p. 404).

[8] This was despite the finding from Green (2020) that 'free school meal pupils received more help from their parents or a family member than did other children' (p. 10).

## Chapter 4

[1] As an aside, my experiences of antenatal care resonate strongly with this assertion: the hospital waiting room for pregnant women I had to frequently attend while expecting my third baby was adorned with multiple posters and a huge upright banner advising women to bond with their baby before birth, through

talking, singing and cuddling them. To quote Lowe et al (2015b, p. 27) 'alongside the cultural image of the foetus, are the twin images of the "perfect mother" who follows expert advice and the "failed" mother who has "taken chances" with her child's future health'.

## Chapter 5

[1]  My eldest daughter returned home in her first term in Year 1 telling me excitedly about 'Dojo points', and how these relate to the class special bear. Here the technologies of old and new discipline are intertwined: if you get 20 points, your name goes in the hat to win the chance to take the cuddly bear home. All week you must perform, just to be in with a chance, but the vast majority of the time, you get no reward at all.

[2]  I make no argument here in relation to the effectiveness of these interventions, which vary hugely from school to school, but aim instead to highlight their symbolic significance.

[3]  In some areas of England a selective system of schools exists still, with pupils taking an 11+ test to determine which secondary school they attend. The Conservative government under Theresa May attempted to expand the use of selective grammar schools in 2016 but had to scale back their plans after concerns were raised about the social impact. In selective areas, the eugenicist idea that we can test children and provide for them differently can be said to be very much in evidence, though the connection with the inflammatory term 'eugenics' is rarely made.

# References

Abi-Rached, J. M. and Rose, N. (2010). The birth of the neuromolecular gaze. *History of the Human Sciences*, 23(1), 11–36.

Adams, R. (2018). Teachers in UK report growing 'vocabulary deficiency', *The Guardian*. Retrieved 7 February 2019, from https://www.theguardian.com/education/2018/apr/19/teachers-in-uk-report-growing-vocabulary-deficiency

Akpan, P. (2020). Black students will suffer most from A-level cancellations – they routinely outperform their predicted grades. Retrieved 7 July 2020, from https://www.independent.co.uk/voices/coronavirus-schools-gcse-a-level-universities-predicted-grades-a9418471.html

Allen, A. (2011). Michael Young's *The Rise of the Meritocracy*: A Philosophical Critique. *British Journal of Educational Studies*, 59(4), 367–382.

Allen, G. (2011a). *Early Intervention: Smart Investment, Massive Savings*. London: HM Government.

Allen, G. (2011b). *Early Intervention: The Next Steps*. London: HM Government.

Allen, G. and Duncan Smith, I. (2008). *Early Intervention: Good Parents, Great Kids, Better Citizens*. London: Centre for Social Justice and Smith Institute.

Annamma, S. A. (2016). *DisCrit: Disability Studies and Critical Race Theory in Education*. New York: Teachers College Press.

Annamma, S. A., Connor, D. and Ferri, B. (2013). Dis/ability critical race studies (DisCrit): Theorizing at the intersections of race and dis/ability. *Race Ethnicity and Education*, 16(1), 1–31.

Annamma, S. A., Ferri, B. A. and Connor, D. J. (2018). Disability critical race theory: Exploring the intersectional lineage, emergence, and potential futures of DisCrit in education. *Review of Research in Education*, 42(1), 46–71.

Archer, L. (2008). The impossibility of minority ethnic educational 'success'? An examination of the discourses of teachers and pupils in British secondary schools. *European Educational Research Journal*, 7(1), 89–107.

Archer, L. and Francis, B. (2007). *Understanding Minority Ethnic Achievement: Debating Race, Gender, Class and 'Success'*. London: Routledge.

Archer, L., Francis, B., Miller, S., Taylor, B., Tereschenko, A., Mazenod, A., Pepper, D. and Travers, M. (2018). The symbolic violence of setting: A Bourdieusian analysis of mixed methods data on secondary students' views about setting. *British Educational Research Journal*, 44(1) 119–140.

Aronsson, L. and Lenz Taguchi, H. (2018). Mapping a collaborative cartography of the encounters between the neurosciences and early childhood education practices. *Discourse: Studies in the Cultural Politics of Education*, 39(2), 242–257.

ATL (2016). Workload drives teacher recruitment and retention crisis. Retrieved 23 March 2017, from https://www.atl.org.uk/latest/press-release/workload-drives-teacher-recruitment-and-retention-crisis-new-survey-finds

Baker, B. (2002). The hunt for disability: The new eugenics and the normalization of school children. *Teachers College Record*, 104(4), 663–703.

Baker, B. (2015). From 'somatic scandals' to 'a constant potential for violence'? The culture of dissection, brain-based learning, and the rewriting/rewiring of 'the child'. *Journal of Curriculum and Pedagogy*, 12(2), 168–197.

Ball, S. (2003). The teacher's soul and the terrors of performativity. *Journal of Education Policy*, 18(2), 215–228.

Ball, S. (2013). *Foucault, Power and Education*. Abingdon: Routledge.

Ball, S. J. (2008). The legacy of ERA, privatization and the policy ratchet. *Educational Management Administration & Leadership*, 36(2), 185–199.

Ball, S. J. (2015). Education, governance and the tyranny of numbers. *Journal of Education Policy*, 30(3), 299–301.

Ball, S. J. (2017). *The Education Debate* (third edition). Bristol: Policy Press.

Ball, S. J. (2018). The banality of numbers. In B. Hamre, A. Morin and C. Ydesen (eds), *Testing and Inclusive Schooling: International Challenges and Opportunities*. Abingdon: Routledge.

BBC News (2018). Help for trauma in childhood 'fragmented'. Retrieved 7 February 2019, from https://www.bbc.co.uk/news/education-46181542

BBC News (2020). Marcus Rashford: Food voucher U-turn after footballer's campaign. Retrieved 27 June 2020, from https://www.bbc.co.uk/news/uk-53065806

Beer, D. (2015). Productive measures: Culture and measurement in the context of everyday neoliberalism. *Big Data & Society*, 2(1), 1–12.

Bei, Z. (in press). No More Exclusions: How a Black-led grassroots coalition movement is answering Coard's Call to Action 50 years on. In B. Richardson (ed), *Tell It Like It Is: How Our Schools Fail Black Children* (third edition). London: Bookmarks.

Bell, D. (1992). *Faces at the Bottom of the Well: The Permanence of Racism*. New York: BasicBooks.

Bibby, T., Lupton, R. and Raffo, C. (2017). *Responding to Poverty and Disadvantage in Schools: A Reader for Teachers*. London: Springer.

Biesta, G. (2017). Education, measurement and the professions: Reclaiming a space for democratic professionality in education. *Educational Philosophy and Theory*, 49(4), 315–330.

Billington, T. (2017). Educational inclusion and critical neuroscience: Friends or foes? *International Journal of Inclusive Education*, 21(8), 866–880.

Blair, T. (2001). Full text of Tony Blair's speech on education. Retrieved 28 June 2020, from https://www.theguardian.com/politics/2001/may/23/labour.tonyblair

Bousted, M. (2020). Ofsted: A problem in search of a solution. *FORUM: For Promoting 3–19 Comprehensive Education*, 62(3), 433–443.

Bradbury, A. (2013a). From model minorities to disposable models: The de-legitimisation of educational success through discourses of authenticity. *Discourse: Studies in the Cultural Politics of Education*, 34(4), 548–561.

Bradbury, A. (2013b). *Understanding Early Years Inequality: Policy, Assessment and Young Children's Identities*. London: Routledge.

Bradbury, A. (2018a). Datafied at four: The role of data in the 'schoolification' of early childhood education in England. *Learning Media and Technology, Special Issue: Datafication of Education*, 44(1), 7–21.

Bradbury, A. (2018b). The impact of the Phonics Screening Check on grouping by ability: A 'necessary evil' amid the policy storm. *British Educational Research Journal*, 44(4), 539–556.

Bradbury, A. (2019a). A critical race theory framework for education policy analysis: The case of bilingual learners and assessment policy in England. *Race Ethnicity and Education*.

Bradbury, A. (2019b). Datafied at four: The role of data in the 'schoolification' of early childhood education in England. *Learning, Media and Technology*, 44(1), 7–21.

Bradbury, A. (2019c). Making little neo-liberals: The production of ideal child/learner subjectivities in primary school through choice, self-improvement and 'growth mindsets'. *Power and Education*, 11(3), 309–326.

Bradbury, A. (2019d). Pressure, Anxiety and Collateral Damage: the Headteachers' Verdict on SATs. Retrieved 7 June 2020, from https://www.morethanascore.org.uk/wp-content/uploads/2019/09/SATs-research.pdf

Bradbury, A. (2019e). Rethinking 'fixed ability thinking' and grouping practices: Questions, disruptions and barriers to change in primary and early years education. *FORUM*, 61(1), 41–52.

Bradbury, A. (2019f). Taking the 'early yearsy' route: Resistance and professionalism in the enactment of assessment policy in early childhood in England. *Education 3–13*, 47(7), 819–830.

Bradbury, A. (2020a). Government and teachers' realities are increasingly worlds apart. Retrieved 1 November 2020, from https://schoolsweek.co.uk/government-and-teachers-realities-are-increasingly-worlds-apart/

Bradbury, A. (2020b). Schools never shut: the extraordinary lengths teachers have been going to in supporting children during lockdown. Retrieved 28 June 2020, from https://blogs.ucl.ac.uk/ioe/2020/06/11/schools-never-shut-the-extraordinary-lengths-teachers-have-been-going-to-in-supporting-children-during-lockdown/

Bradbury, A. and Duncan, S. (2020). Choosing welfare over worksheets and care over 'catch-up': teachers' priorities during lockdown. Retrieved 7 July 2020, from https://blogs.ucl.ac.uk/ioe/2020/07/03/choosing-welfare-over-worksheets-and-care-over-catch-up-teachers-priorities-during-lockdown/

Bradbury, A. and Roberts-Holmes, G. (2017a). Creating an Ofsted story: The role of early years assessment data in schools' narratives of progress. *British Journal of Sociology of Education*, 38(7), 943–955.

Bradbury, A. and Roberts-Holmes, G. (2017b). *Grouping in Early Years and Key Stage 1: A 'Necessary Evil'?* London: National Education Union.

Bradbury, A. and Roberts-Holmes, G. (2017c). *The Datafication of Early Years and Primary Education: Playing with Numbers.* London: Routledge

Bradbury, A., Wyse, D. and Manyukhina, Y. (2020). HHCP Submission to the House of Lords *Life after Covid* Committee.

Bradford, S. and Hey, V. (2007). Successful subjectivities? The successification of class, ethnic and gender positions. *Journal of Education Policy*, 22(6), 595–614.

Braun, A. and Maguire, M. (2020) Doing without believing – enacting policy in the English primary school. *Critical Studies in Education*, 61(4), 433–447.

Breiter, A. (2016). *Datafication in education: A multi-level challenge for IT in educational management*. Paper presented at the International Conference on Stakeholders and Information Technology in Education.

Broer, T. and Pickersgill, M. (2015a). (Low) expectations, legitimization, and the contingent uses of scientific knowledge: Engagements with neuroscience in Scottish social policy and services. *Engaging Science, Technology, and Society*, 1, 47–66.

Broer, T. and Pickersgill, M. (2015b). Targeting brains, producing responsibilities: The use of neuroscience within British social policy. *Social Science & Medicine*, 132, 54–61.

Bromley, M. (2018). Pupil Premium: Closing the vocabulary gap (SecEd). Retrieved 7 February 2019, from http://www.sec-ed.co.uk/best-practice/pupil-premium-closing-the-vocabulary-gap/

Brown, C. (2017). 'Favourite places in school' for lower-set 'ability' pupils: School groupings practices and children's spatial orientations. *Children's Geographies*, 15(4), 399–412.

Bruer, J. T. (1999). *The Myth of the First Three Years: A New Understanding of Early Brain Development and Lifelong Learning*. New York, NY: Simon and Schuster.

Burns, J. (2020). Schools give emergency food to families with nothing to eat. Retrieved 5 July 2020, from https://www.bbc.co.uk/news/education-52325332

Busso, D. S. and Pollack, C. (2015). No brain left behind: Consequences of neuroscience discourse for education. *Learning, Media and Technology*, 40(2), 168–186.

Butler, J. (2010). *Frames of War: When Is Life Grievable?* New York, NY: Verso.

Byrd, J. (2020). Imagining a 'new normal' free from judgement and blame: Creating sustainable partnerships with students and parents. *FORUM: For Promoting 3–19 Comprehensive Education* 62(3), 345–352.

Campbell, T. (2013). *In-school Ability Grouping and the Month of Birth Effect. Preliminary Evidence from the Millenium Cohort Study.* London: Centre for Longitudinal Studies.

Campbell, T. (2014). Stratified at seven: In-class ability grouping and the relative age effect. *British Educational Research Journal*, 40(5), 749–771.

Carr, J. (2020). Coronavirus: Over half of laptops STILL to be delivered in just two weeks. Retrieved 5 July 2020, from https://schoolsweek. co.uk/coronavirus-over-half-of-laptops-still-to-be-delivered-in-just-two-weeks/

Casciani, D. (2020). Home schooling: The Zoom haves and have nots. Retrieved 14 June 2020, from https://www.bbc.co.uk/news/ education-52761068

Child Welfare Information Gateway (n.d.). Trauma-Informed Practice. Retrieved 7 February 2019, from https://www.childwelfare.gov/ topics/responding/trauma/

Children's Commissioner (2020). We're all in this together? Local area profiles of child vulnerability. Retrieved 9 July 2020, from https:// www.childrenscommissioner.gov.uk/wp-content/uploads/2020/04/ cco-were-all-in-this-together.pdf

Chitty, C. (2007). *Eugenics, Race and Intelligence in Education*. London: Bloomsbury Publishing.

Chitty, C. (2011). Differing views of human intelligence. *FORUM: For Promoting 3–19 Comprehensive Education*, 52(3) 235–246.

Civinini, C. (2020). Heads vote to scrap 'nonsensical' 2021 Sats. Retrieved 21 October 2020, from https://www.tes.com/news/ heads-vote-scrap-nonsensical-2021-sats

Coard, B. (1971). *How the West Indian Child Is Made Educationally Subnormal in the British School System: The Scandal of the Black Child in Schools in Britain*. London: New Beacon for the Caribbean Education and Community Workers' Association.

Coldron, J., Crawford, M., Jones, S. and Simkins, T. (2014). The restructuring of schooling in England: The responses of well-positioned headteachers. *Educational Management Administration & Leadership*, 42(3), 387–403.

Connor, D. J. and Ferri, B. A. (2007). The conflict within: Resistance to inclusion and other paradoxes in special education. *Disability & Society*, 22(1), 63–77.

Conservative Party (2010). Conservative Party Manifesto. Retrieved 19 December 2012, from http://media.conservatives.s3.amazonaws. com/manifesto/cpmanifesto2010_lowres.pdf

Conservative Party (2019). Our Plan – Conservative Manifesto 2019. Retrieved 28 June 2020, from https://www.conservatives.com/ our-plan

Corrie, L. (2000). Neuroscience and early childhood? A dangerous liaison. *Australian Journal of Early Childhood*, 25(2), 34–40.

Coughlan, S. (2020). Free internet to help poorer pupils study online. Retrieved 5 July 2020, from https://www.bbc.co.uk/news/education-53057767

Dahlberg, G. and Moss, P. (2005). *Ethics and Politics in Early Childhood Education.* London: RoutledgeFalmer.

D'Arcy, K. (2014). Home education, school, Travellers and educational inclusion. *British Journal of Sociology of Education*, 35(5), 818–835.

Davis, A. (2004). The credentials of brain-based learning. *Journal of Philosophy of Education*, 38(1), 21–36.

De Vos, J. (2016). The death and the resurrection of (psy) critique: The case of neuroeducation. *Foundations of Science*, 21(1), 129–145.

De Vos, J. (2017). The neuroturn in education: Between the Scylla of psychologization and the Charybdis of digitalization? In M. VandenBroeck (ed), *Constructions of Neuroscience in Early Childhood Education* (pp. 30–46). Abingdon: Routledge.

De Vos, J. and Pluth, E. (2015). (eds) *Neuroscience and Critique: Exploring the Limits of the Neurological Turn.* London: Routledge.

Delgado, R. and Stefancic, J. (2000). *Critical Race Theory: The Cutting Edge.* Philadelphia, PA: Temple University Press.

Demie, F. and Lewis, K. (2011). White working class achievement: An ethnographic study of barriers to learning in schools. *Educational Studies*, 37(3), 245–264.

DfE (2013). Written statement to Parliament: Pupil premium funding. Retrieved 28 April 2015, from https://www.gov.uk/government/speeches/pupil-premium-funding

DfE (2016). Progress 8: How Progress 8 and Attainment 8 measures are calculated. Retrieved 6 July 2020, from https://assets.publishing.service.gov.uk/government/uploads/system/uploads/attachment_data/file/561021/Progress_8_and_Attainment_8_how_measures_are_calculated.pdf

DfE (2017a). Nick Gibb: The importance of knowledge-based education. Retrieved 20 October 2020, from https://www.gov.uk/government/speeches/nick-gibb-the-importance-of-knowledge-based-education

DfE (2017b). Primary assessment public consultations: Government response. Retrieved 23 March 2018, from https://www.gov.uk/government/speeches/primary-assessment-public-consultations-government-response

DfE (2017c). Statutory Framework for the Early Years Foundation Stage. Retrieved 7 January 2021, from https://www.foundationyears.org.uk/files/2017/03/EYFS_STATUTORY_FRAMEWORK_2017.pdf

DfE (2018). Multi-million fund to boost children's early language skills. Retrieved 7 February 2019, from https://www.gov.uk/government/news/multi-million-fund-to-boost-childrens-early-language-skills

Dixson, A. and Rousseau, C. (2006). *Critical Race Theory in Education: All God's Children Got a Song.* New York, NY: Taylor & Francis.

Dorling, D. and Tomlinson, S. (2016). The creation of inequality: Myths of potential and ability. *Journal of Critical Education Policy Studies*, 14(3), 56–79.

Drummond, M. J. and Yarker, P. (2013). The enduring problem of fixed ability: But is a new conversation beginning? *FORUM: For Promoting 3–19 Comprehensive Education*, 55(1), 3–7.

Dumit, J. (2015). Afterword. In J. De Vos and E. Pluth (eds), *Neuroscience and Critique: Exploring the Limits of the Neurological Turn* (pp. 221–229). London: Routledge.

Dunne, M., Humphreys, S., Dyson, A., Sebba, J., Gallannaugh, F. and Muijs, D. (2011). The teaching and learning of pupils in low-attainment sets. *The Curriculum Journal*, 22(4), 485–513.

Edwards, R., Gillies, V. and Horsley, N. (2015). Brain science and early years policy: Hopeful ethos or 'cruel optimism'? *Critical Social Policy*, 35(2), 167–187.

EEF (2020). Online tuition pilot launched as new EEF analysis finds school closures could undo recent progress on closing the attainment gap. Retrieved 14 June 2020, from https://educationendowmentfoundation.org.uk/news/online-tuition-pilot-launched-school-closures-could-undo-progress/

Eynon, R. (2013). The rise of Big Data: What does it mean for education, technology, and media research? *Learning, Media and Technology*, 38(3), 237–240.

Fias, W. (2017). The complexity of translating neuroscience to education: The case of number processing. In M. Vandenbroeck (ed), *Constructions of Neuroscience in Early Childhood Education* (pp. 68–81). Abingdon: Routledge.

Fletcher, R. (2011). *Intelligence and Intelligence Testing.* London: Routledge.

Foucault, M. (1977). *Discipline and Punish: The Birth of the Prison.* London: Allen Lane.

Foucault, M. (1982). The subject and power. *Critical inquiry*, 8(4), 777–795.

Francis, B. and Skelton, C. (2005). *Reassessing Gender and Achievement: Questioning Contemporary Key Debates.* London: Routledge.

Francis, B., Archer, L., Hodgen, J., Pepper, D., Taylor, B. and Travers, M.-C. (2017). Exploring the relative lack of impact of research on 'ability grouping' in England: A discourse analytic account. *Cambridge Journal of Education*, 47(1), 1–17.

Francis, B., Craig, N., Hodgen, J., Taylor, B., Tereshchenko, A., Connolly, P., and Archer, L. (2020). The impact of tracking by attainment on pupil self-confidence over time: Demonstrating the accumulative impact of self-fulfilling prophecy. *British Journal of Sociology of Education*, 41(5), 626–642.

Francis, B., Taylor, B. and Tereshchenko, A. (2019). *Reassessing 'Ability' Grouping: Improving Practice for Equity and Attainment*. Abingdon: Routledge.

Freedman, J. and Ferri, B. A. (2017). Locating the problem within: Race, learning disabilities, and science. *Teachers College Record*, 19(5), 1–28.

Gewirtz, S. (2002). *The Managerial School: Post-welfarism and Social Justice in Education*. London: Routledge.

Gewirtz, S., Maguire, M., Neumann, E. and Towers, E. (2019). What's wrong with 'deliverology'? Performance measurement, accountability and quality improvement in English secondary education. *Journal of Education Policy*, 1–26.

Gillborn, D. (2006a). Critical race theory and education: Racism and anti-racism in educational theory and praxis. *Discourse: Studies in the Cultural Politics of Education*, 27(1), 11–32.

Gillborn, D. (2006b). Rethinking white supremacy: who counts in 'Whiteworld'. *Ethnicities*, 6(3), 318–340.

Gillborn, D. (2008). *Racism and Education: Coincidence or Conspiracy?* London: Routledge.

Gillborn, D. (2009). Education: The numbers game and the construction of white racial victimhood. In K. Sveinsson (ed), *Who Cares About the White Working Class?* (pp. 15–22). London: Runnymede Trust.

Gillborn, D. (2010). Reform, racism and the centrality of whiteness: Assessment, ability and the 'new eugenics'. *Irish Educational Studies*, 29(3), 231–252.

Gillborn, D. (2013). Interest-divergence and the colour of cutbacks: Race, recession and the undeclared war on Black children. *Discourse: Studies in the Cultural Politics of Education*, 34(4), 477–491.

Gillborn, D. (2016). Softly, softly: Genetics, intelligence and the hidden racism of the new geneism. *Journal of Education Policy*, 31(4), 365–388.

Gillborn, D. (2018). Heads I win, tails you lose: Anti-Black racism as fluid, relentless, individual and systemic. *Peabody Journal of Education*, 93(1), 66–77.

Gillborn, D. and Youdell, D. (2000). *Rationing Education: Policy, Practice, Reform and Equity.* Buckingham: Open University Press.

Gillborn, D. and Youdell, D. (2001). The new IQism: Intelligence, 'ability' and the rationing of education. In J. Demaine (ed), *Sociology of Education Today.* London: Palgrave Macmillan.

Gillborn, D., Demack, S., Rollock, N. and Warmington, P. (2017). Moving the goalposts: Education policy and 25 years of the Black/White achievement gap. *British Educational Research Journal*, 43(5), 848–874.

Gillborn, D., Warmington, P. and Demack, S. (2018). QuantCrit: Education, policy, 'Big Data' and principles for a critical race theory of statistics. *Race Ethnicity and Education*, 21(2), 158–179.

Gillies, V., Edwards, R. and Horsley, N. (2017). *Challenging the Politics of Early Intervention: Who's 'Saving' Children and Why?* Bristol: Policy Press.

Giordano, C. (2020). Boris Johnson says attacking statues is 'lying about our history' and protests have been 'hijacked by extremists'. Retrieved 14 June 2020, from https://www.independent.co.uk/news/uk/politics/boris-johnson-statues-churchill-mandela-colston-protests-black-lives-matter-a9562626.html

Gitelman, L. and Jackson, V. (2013). *'Raw Data' Is an Oxymoron.* Cambridge, MA: MIT Press.

Gore, J. M. (1995). On the continuity of power relations in pedagogy. *International Studies in Sociology of Education*, 5(2), 165–188.

Gore, J. M. (2001). Disciplining bodies: On the continuity of power relations in pedagogy. In Paechter, C. (Ed.). (2001). *Learning, space and identity* London: Paul Chapman 167–181.

Goswami, U. (2004). Neuroscience and education. *British Journal of Educational Psychology*, 74, 1–14.

Goswami, U. (2006). Neuroscience and education: From research to practice? *Nature Reviews: Neuroscience*, 7, 406–413.

Graue, E. (2006). The answer is readiness – now what is the question? *Early Education and Development*, 17(1), 43–56.

Green, F. (2020). LLAKES Research Paper 67 Schoolwork in lockdown: new evidence on the epidemic of educational poverty. Retrieved 5 July 2020, from https://www.llakes.ac.uk/sites/default/files/LLAKES%20Working%20Paper%2067_0.pdf

Grimaldi, E., Landri, P. and Taglietti, D. (2020). For a public sociology of digital schooling. Retrieved 7 July 2020, from https://irs-blog.com/2020/07/06/for-a-public-sociology-of-digital-schooling-emiliano-grimaldi-paolo-landri-and-danilo-taglietti/

Gulson, K. N. and Baker, B. M. (2018). New biological rationalities in education. *Discourse: Studies in the Cultural Politics of Education*, 39(2), 159–168.

Gulson, K. N. and Sellar, S. (2018). Emerging data infrastructures and the new topologies of education policy. *Environment and Planning D: Society and Space*, 37 (2) 350–366.

Gulson, K. N. and Webb, P. T. (2018). 'Life' and education policy: Intervention, augmentation and computation. *Discourse: Studies in the Cultural Politics of Education*, 39(2), 276–291.

Hamilton, L. and O'Hara, P. (2011). The tyranny of setting (ability grouping): Challenges to inclusion in Scottish primary schools. *Teaching and Teacher Education*, 27(4), 712–721.

Hardy, I. (2014). A logic of appropriation: Enacting national testing (NAPLAN) in Australia. *Journal of Education Policy*, 29(1), 1–18.

Hardy, I. (2015). 'I'm just a numbers person': The complexity, nature and effects of the quantification of education. *International Studies in Sociology of Education*, 25(1), 20–37.

Hardy, I. (2021). The quandary of quantification: Data, numbers and teachers' learning. *Journal of Education Policy*, 36(1), 44–63.

Hargreaves, E., Quick, L. and Buchanan, D. (2021). 'I got rejected': Investigating the status of 'low-attaining' children in primary-schooling. *Pedagogy, Culture & Society*, 29(1), 79–97.

Harmey, S. and Moss, G. (2020) Learning loss versus learning disruption: Written evidence submitted to the Education Select Committee Inquiry into the impact of COVID-19. London: UCL Institute of Education.

Haslam-Ormerod, S. (2019). 'Snowflake millennial' label is inaccurate and reverses progress to destigmatise mental health. Retrieved 14 June 2019, from https://theconversation.com/snowflake-millennial-label-is-inaccurate-and-reverses-progress-to-destigmatise-mental-health-109667

Haye, A., Matus, C., Cottet, P. and Niño, S. (2018). Autonomy and the ambiguity of biological rationalities: Systems theory, ADHD and Kant. *Discourse: Studies in the Cultural Politics of Education*, 39(2), 184–195.

Hayles, F. (2020). How to help primary children reintegrate after lockdown. Retrieved 1 November 2020, from https://www.tes.com/news/schools-reopening-september-coronavirus-how-help-children-reintegrate

Hinds, D. (2018). Education Secretary sets vision for boosting social mobility. Retrieved 7 February 2019, from https://www.gov.uk/government/speeches/education-secretary-sets-vision-for-boosting-social-mobility

Hinds, D. (2019). Letter to all Academy Trusts and Local Authorities: Reducing Workloads – Making Data Work in Schools. Retrieved 21 June 2020, from https://assets.publishing.service.gov. uk/government/uploads/system/uploads/attachment_data/file/817713/Data_burdens_on_schools.pdf

HoC Science and Technology Committee (2018). Evidence-based early years intervention. Retrieved 25 January 2019, from https://publications.parliament.uk/pa/cm201719/cmselect/cmsctech/506/506.pdf

Holloway, J. and Brass, J. (2018). Making accountable teachers: The terrors and pleasures of performativity. *Journal of Education Policy*, 33(3), 361–382.

Howard-Jones, P. A. (2011). From brain scan to lesson plan. *Psychologist*, 24(2), 110–113.

IFS (2020). Learning during the lockdown: real-time data on children's experiences during home learning. Retrieved 6 July 2020, from https://www.ifs.org.uk/publications/14848

International Literacy Centre (ILC) (2020a). Responding to COVID-19, Briefing Note 1: Primary Assessment and COVID. London: UCL Institute of Education.

International Literacy Centre (ILC) (2020b). Responding to COVID-19, Briefing Note 2: Learning after lockdown. London: UCL Institute of Education.

International Literacy Centre (ILC) (2020c). Responding to COVID-19, Briefing Note 3: Resetting educational priorities in challenging times. London: UCL Institute of Education.

Ireson, J. and Hallam, S. (2001). *Ability Grouping in Education*. London: Sage.

Jackson, C. (2006). 'Wild' girls? An exploration of 'ladette' cultures in secondary schools. *Gender and Education*, 18(4), 339–360.

Jackson, P. (2014). The crisis of the 'disadvantaged child': Poverty research, IQ, and muppet diplomacy in the 1960s. *Antipode*, 46(1), 190–208.

Jarke, J. and Breiter, A. (2019a). Editorial: The datafication of education. *Learning, Media and Technology*, 44(1), 1–6.

Jarke, J. and Breiter, A. (2019b). *The Datafication of Education*. London: Taylor & Francis.

Jennings, J. (2012). The effects of accountability system design on teachers' use of test score data. *Teachers College Record*, 114(11), 1–23.

Jin, J. and Ball, S. J. (2020). Meritocracy, social mobility and a new form of class domination. *British Journal of Sociology of Education*, 41(1), 64–79.

Keddie, A. (2015). 'We haven't done enough for White working-class children': Issues of distributive justice and ethnic identity politics. *Race Ethnicity and Education*, 18(4), 515–534.

Keddie, A. (2016). Children of the market: Performativity, neoliberal responsibilisation and the construction of student identities. *Oxford Review of Education*, 42(1), 108–122.

Keddie, A. (2017). Primary school leadership in England: Performativity and matters of professionalism. *British Journal of Sociology of Education*, 38(8), 1245–1257.

Kitchen, W. H. (2017). *A Philosophical Critique of Neuroscience and Education*. London: Bloomsbury Academic.

Kitchin, R. (2014). *The Data Revolution: Big Data, Open Data, Data Infrastructures & Their Consequences*. London: Sage.

Labour Party (2019). Manifesto: Rebuild our Public Services. Retrieved 28 June 2020, from https://labour.org.uk/manifesto-2019/rebuild-our-public-services/

Ladson-Billings, G. (2004). Just what is Critical Race Theory and what's it doing in a *nice* field like education? In G. Ladson-Billings and D. Gillborn (eds), *The RoutledgeFalmer Reader in Multicultural Education*. Abingdon: RoutledgeFalmer.

Ladwig, J. G. and McPherson, A. (2017). The anatomy of ability. *Curriculum Inquiry*, 47(4), 344–362.

Lee, S. (2008). Foreword. In G. Li and L. Wang (eds), *Model Minority Myth Revisited: An Interdisciplinary Approach to Demystifying Asian American Educational Experiences* (pp. ix–xi). Charlotte, NC: Information Age Publishers.

Leonardo, Z. and Broderick, A. (2011). Smartness as property: A critical exploration of intersections between whiteness and disability studies. *Teachers College Record*, 113(10), 2206–2232.

Lewis, P. and Bosely, S. (2010). Iain Duncan Smith 'distorted' research on childhood neglect and brain size. *The Guardian*. Retrieved 31 January 2013, from http://www.guardian.co.uk/politics/2010/apr/09/iain-duncan-smith-childrens-brains

Lingard, B. and Sellar, S. (2013). 'Catalyst data': Perverse systemic effects of audit and accountability in Australian schooling. *Journal of Education Policy*, 28(5), 634–656.

Lingard, B., Martino, W. and Rezai-Rashti, G. (2013). Testing regimes, accountabilities and education policy: Commensurate global and national developments. *Journal of Education Policy*, 28(5), 539–556.

Littler, J. (2017). *Against Meritocracy: Culture, Power and Myths of Mobility*. London: Routledge.

Lough, C. (2020a). Analysis: Are teacher-assessed GCSE grades a good idea? Retrieved 7 July 2020, from https://www.tes.com/news/analysis-are-teacher-assessed-gcse-grades-good-idea

Lough, C. (2020b). Ofsted to inspect schools on Covid catch-up plans. Retrieved 28 June 2020, from https://www.tes.com/news/coronavirus-ofsted-inspect-schools-covid-catch-plans

Lowe, P., Lee, E. and Macvarish, J. (2015a). Biologising parenting: Neuroscience discourse, English social and public health policy and understandings of the child. *Sociology of Health & Illness*, 37(2), 198–211.

Lowe, P., Lee, E. and Macvarish, J. (2015b). Growing better brains? Pregnancy and neuroscience discourses in English social and welfare policies. *Health, Risk & Society*, 17(1), 15–29.

Lowe, R. (1997). *Schooling and Social Change, 1964–1990*. London: Psychology Press.

Lupton, D. and Williamson, B. (2017). The datafied child: The dataveillance of children and implications for their rights. *New Media & Society*, 19(5), 780–794.

Lynch, T. L. (2015). *Hidden Role of Software in Educational Research: Policy to Practice*. London: Routledge.

MacGilchrist, F. (2019). Cruel optimism in edtech: When the digital data practices of educational technology providers inadvertently hinder educational equity. *Learning, Media and Technology*, 44(1), 77–86.

MacNaughton, G. (2004). The politics of logic in early childhood research: A case of the brain, hard facts, trees and rhizomes. *The Australian Educational Researcher*, 31(3), 87–104.

MacPherson, W. (1999). *The Stephen Lawrence Inquiry*. London: The Stationery Office.

Manolev, J., Sullivan, A. and Slee, R. (2019). The datafication of discipline: ClassDojo, surveillance and a performative classroom culture. *Learning, Media and Technology*, 44(1), 36–51.

Manovich, L. (2012). Trending: The promises and challenges of big social data. In M. Gold (ed), *Debates in the Digital Humanities*. Minnesota, MN: University of Minnesota Press.

Manovich, L. (2013). *Software Takes Command: Extending the Language of New Media*. New York, NY: Bloomsbury Academic.

Mansfield, B. and Guthman, J. (2015). Epigenetic life: Biological plasticity, abnormality, and new configurations of race and reproduction. *Cultural Geographies*, 22(1), 3–20.

Marks, R. (2013). 'The blue table means you don't have a clue': the persistence of fixed-ability thinking and practices in primary mathematics in English schools. *FORUM: For Promoting 3–19 Comprehensive Education*, 55(1), 31–44.

Marks, R. (2014). Educational triage and ability-grouping in primary mathematics: A case-study of the impacts on low-attaining pupils. *Research in Mathematics Education*, 16(1), 38–53.

Marks, R. (2016). *Ability-grouping in Primary Schools: Case Studies and Critical Debates*. Northwich: Critical Publishing.

Mason, R. and Sample, I. (2020). Sabisky row: Dominic Cummings criticised over 'designer babies' post. Retrieved 14 June 2020, from https://www.theguardian.com/politics/2020/feb/19/sabisky-row-dominic-cummings-criticised-over-designer-babies-post

May, T. (2016a). Britain, the great meritocracy: Prime Minister's speech. Retrieved 24 August 2017, from https://www.gov.uk/government/speeches/britain-the-great-meritocracy-prime-ministers-speech

May, T. (2016b). Statement from the new Prime Minister Theresa May. Retrieved 28 June 2020, from https://www.gov.uk/government/speeches/statement-from-the-new-prime-minister-theresa-may

Mayor, C. (2018). Whitewashing trauma: Applying neoliberalism, governmentality, and whiteness theory to trauma training for teachers. *Whiteness and Education*, 3(2), 198–216.

McCulloch, G. (2016). British Labour Party education policy and comprehensive education: From Learning to Live to Circular 10/65. *History of Education*, 45(2), 225–245.

McGillicuddy, D. and Devine, D. (2018). 'Turned off' or 'ready to fly' – Ability grouping as an act of symbolic violence in primary school. *Teaching and Teacher Education*, 70, 88–99.

McGillicuddy, D. and Devine, D. (2020). 'You feel ashamed that you are not in the higher group' – Children's psychosocial response to ability grouping in primary school. *British Educational Research Journal*, 46(3), 553–573.

McGimpsey, I. (2016). Late neoliberalism: Delineating a policy regime. *Critical Social Policy*, 37(1), 64–84.

McGimpsey, I., Bradbury, A. and Santori, D. (2017). Revisions to rationality: The translation of 'new knowledges' into policy under the Coalition Government. *British Journal of Sociology of Education*, 38(6), 908–925.

Meloni, M. (2017). Race in an epigenetic time: Thinking biology in the plural. *The British Journal of Sociology*, 68(3), 389–409.

Migliarini, V. (2018). 'Colour-evasiveness' and racism without race: The disablement of asylum-seeking children at the edge of fortress Europe. *Race Ethnicity and Education*, 21(4), 438–457.

Migliarini, V., D'Alessio, S. and Bocci, F. (2020). SEN policies and migrant children in Italian schools: micro-exclusions through discourses of equality. *Discourse: Studies in the Cultural Politics of Education*, 41(6), 887–900.

Millar, F. (2020). It's still rich v poor in English schools – exactly as Boris Johnson likes it. Retrieved 10 June 2020, from https://www.theguardian.com/education/2020/jun/09/its-still-rich-v-poor-in-english-schools-exactly-as-boris-johnson-likes-it?CMP=Share_AndroidApp_Outlook

Millei, Z. and Joronen, M. (2016). The (bio)politicization of neuroscience in Australian early years policies: Fostering brain-resources as human capital. *Journal of Education Policy*, 31(4), 389–404.

Mirza, H. S. and Meetoo, V. (2018). Empowering Muslim girls? Post-feminism, multiculturalism and the production of the 'model' Muslim female student in British schools. *British Journal of Sociology of Education*, 39(2), 227–241.

Monroe, J. (2020). The free school meals row should open up a debate about poverty itself. Retrieved 1 November 2020, from https://www.theguardian.com/commentisfree/2020/oct/26/ffree-school-meals-row-debate-poverty-desperate-situations

More than a Score (2020). Cancel SATs and all formal government tests in primary schools in 2021. Retrieved 28 June 2020, from https://actionnetwork.org/petitions/cancel-sats-and-all-formal-government-tests-in-primary-schools-in-2021?source=direct_link&

Morning, A. (2014). And you thought we had moved beyond all that: Biological race returns to the social sciences. *Ethnic and Racial Studies*, 37(10), 1676–1685.

Moss, G. (2020a). Are free school meals about wellbeing … or attainment? Retrieved 1 November 2020, from https://www.tes.com/news/are-free-school-meals-about-wellbeingor-attainment

Moss, G. (2020b). Education in the Time of COVID-19 – Rebuild, Reconnect, Reimagine. Retrieved 1 November 2020, from https://blogs.ucl.ac.uk/ceid/2020/09/02/moss/

Moss, G., Allen, R., Bradbury, A., Duncan, S., Harmey, S. and Levy, R. (2020). *Primary Teachers' Experience of the COVID-19 Lockdown – Eight Key Messages for Policymakers Going Forward*. London: UCL Institute of Education.

Moss, P. (2015). There are alternatives! Contestation and hope in early childhood education. *Global Studies of Childhood*, 5(3), 226–238.

Moullin, S., Waldfogel, J. and Washbrook, E. (2014). Baby bonds: Parenting, attachment and a secure base for children. Retrieved 6 January 2021, from https://www.suttontrust.com/our-research/baby-bonds-early-years/

Mroz, A. (2020). We mustn't waste the opportunity Covid-19 has given us. Retrieved 8 July 2020, from https://www.tes.com/magazine/article/we-mustnt-waste-opportunity-covid-19-has-given-us

Muijs, D. and Dunne, M. (2010). Setting by ability – or is it? A quantitative study of determinants of set placement in English secondary schools. *Educational Research*, 52(4), 391–407.

Murphy, R. and Wyness, G. (2020). Minority Report: The impact of predicted grades on university admissions of disadvantaged groups. *Education Economics*, 28(4), 333–350.

Murray, C. (2014). Book Review: 'A Troublesome Inheritance' by Nicholas Wade. Retrieved 14 June 2020, from https://www.wsj.com/articles/book-review-a-troublesome-inheritance-by-nicholas-wade-1399066489?tesla=y

Myers, M., McGhee, D. and Bhopal, K. (2010). At the crossroads: Gypsy and Traveller parents' perceptions of education, protection and social change. *Race Ethnicity and Education*, 13(4), 533–548.

Neaum, S. (2016). School readiness and pedagogies of Competence and Performance: Theorising the troubled relationship between early years and early years policy. *International Journal of Early Years Education*, 24(3), 239–253.

NEU (2020). Covid19 – Understanding and dealing with the traumatic effects of the pandemic on your students. Retrieved 28 June 2020, from https://neu.org.uk/online-cpd/covid19-understanding-and-dealing-traumatic-effects-pandemic-your-students

Neumann, E. (2021). Setting by numbers: Datafication processes and ability grouping in an English secondary school. *Journal of Education Policy*, 36(1), 1–23.

OECD (2008). *Understanding the Brain: the Birth of a Learning Science.* Paris: OECD.

Omi, M. and Winant, H. (2004). On the theoretical status of the concept of race. In G. Ladson-Billings and D. Gillborn (eds), *The RoutledgeFalmer Reader in Multicultural Education: Critical Perspectives on Race, Racism and Education* (pp. 7–15). London: RoutledgeFalmer.

OUP (2018). Why Closing the Word Gap Matters: Oxford Language Report. Retrieved 7 February 2019, from https://global.oup.com/education/content/dictionaries/key-issues/word-gap/?region=uk

Ozga, J. (2009). Governing education through data in England: From regulation to self-evaluation. *Journal of Education Policy*, 24(2), 149–162.

Ozga, J., Dahler-Larsen, P., Segerholm, C. and Simola, H. (eds) (2011). *Fabricating Quality in Education: Data and Governance in Europe*. London: Routledge.

Parsons, C. (2009). Explaining sustained inequalities in ethnic minority school exclusions in England – Passive racism in a neoliberal grip. *Oxford Review of Education*, 35(2), 249–265.

Peck, J. and Tickell, A. (2002). Neoliberalizing space. *Antipode*, 34, 380–404.

Penn, H. (2017). Anything to divert attention from poverty. In M. Vandenbroeck (ed), *Constructions of Neuroscience in Early Childhood Education* (pp. 54–67). Abingdon: Routledge.

Perryman, J. (2006). Panoptic performativity and school inspection regimes: Disciplinary mechanisms and life under special measures. *Journal of Education Policy*, 21(2), 147–161.

Piattoeva, N. (2015). Elastic numbers: National examinations data as a technology of government. *Journal of Education Policy*, 30(3), 316–334.

Pickersgill, M. (2018). *The Value of the Imagined Biological in Policy and Society: Somaticizing and Economizing British Subject(ivitie)s*. London: Routledge.

Popkewitz, T. S. (2012). Numbers in grids of intelligibility: Making sense of how educational truth is told. In H. Lauder, M. Young, H. Daniels, M. Balarin and J. Lowe (eds), *Educating for the Knowledge Economy? Critical Perspectives* (pp. 169–191). Abingdon: Routledge.

Pratt, N. (2016). Neoliberalism and the (internal) marketisation of primary school assessment in England. *British Educational Research Journal*, 42(5), 890–905.

Pratt, N. and Alderton, J. (2019). Producing assessment truths: A Foucauldian analysis of teachers' reorganisation of levels in English primary schools. *British Journal of Sociology of Education*, 40(5), 581–597.

Purdy, N. and Morrison, H. (2009). Cognitive neuroscience and education: Unravelling the confusion. *Oxford Review of Education*, 35(1), 99–109.

Pykett, J. (2012). Neurocapitalism and the new neuros: Using neuroeconomics, behavioural economics and picoeconomics for public policy. *Journal of Economic Geography*, 13(5), 845–869.

Ratner, H., Andersen, B. L. and Madsen, S. R. (2019). Configuring the teacher as data user: Public-private sector mediations of national test data. *Learning, Media and Technology*, 44(1), 22–35.

Reay, D. (2006). The zombie stalking English schools: Social class and educational inequality. *British Journal of Educational Studies*, 54(3), 288–307.

Reay, D. (2017). *Miseducation: Inequality, Education and the Working Classes*. Bristol: Policy Press.

Reay, D. (2020a). English education in the time of coronavirus. *FORUM: For Promoting 3–19 Comprehensive Education*, 62(3) 311–322.

Reay, D. (2020b). The perils and penalties of meritocracy: Sanctioning inequalities and legitimating prejudice. *The Political Quarterly*, 91(2), 405–412.

Rethinking Assessment (2020). About us: Our Advisory Group for Rethinking Assessment. Retrieved 21 October 2020, from https://rethinkingassessment.com/about-us-ra/

Richardson, K. (2017). *Genes, Brains, and Human Potential: The Science and Ideology of Intelligence*. New York, NY: Columbia University Press.

Roberts, J. (2020). Minister accused of demonising families on FSM vouchers. Retrieved 8 July 2020, from https://www.tes.com/news/coronavirus-minister-accused-demonising-families-fsm-vouchers

Roberts-Holmes, G. (2015). The 'datafication' of early years pedagogy: If the teaching is good, the data should be good and if there's bad teaching, there is bad data'. *Journal of Education Policy*, 30(3), 302–315.

Roberts-Holmes, G. (2019). School readiness, governance and early years ability grouping. *Contemporary Issues in Early Childhood*, https://doi.org/10.1177/1463949119863128.

Roberts-Holmes, G. and Bradbury, A. (2016). Governance, accountability and the datafication of early years education in England. *British Education Research Journal*, 42(4), 600–613.

Roberts-Holmes, G., Lee., S.-F., Sousa, D. and Jones, E. (2020). Research into the 2019 Pilot of Reception Baseline Assessment. Retrieved 7 July 2020, from https://neu.org.uk/media/9116/view

Roderick, M. (2012). Drowning in data but thirsty for analysis. *Teachers College Record*, 114(11), 1–9.

Rollock, N., Gillborn, D., Vincent, C. and Ball, S. (2015). *The Colour of Class*. London: Routledge.

Rose, H. and Rose, S. (2012). *Genes, Cells and Brains: Bioscience's Promethean Promises*. London: Verso.

Rose, N. (2001). The politics of life itself. *Theory, Culture & Society*, 18(6), 1–30.

Rose, N. (2007). *Politics of Life Itself: Biomedicine, Power and Subjectivity in the Twenty-first Century*. Princeton, NJ, Oxford: Princeton University Press.

Rose, N. (2010). 'Screen and intervene': Governing risky brains. *History of the Human Sciences*, 23(1), 79–105.

Roxby, P. (2020). Coronavirus: Child psychologists highlight mental health risks of lockdown. Retrieved 6 July 2020, from https://www.bbc.co.uk/news/health-53037702

Scherer, L. (2016). 'I am not clever, they are cleverer than us': Children reading in the primary school. *British Journal of Sociology of Education*, 37(3), 389–407.

Scheurich, J. J. (1994). Policy archaeology: A new policy studies methodology. *Journal of Education Policy*, 9(4), 297–316.

Selwyn, N. (2016a). *Is Technology Good for Education?* Cambridge: Polity.

Selwyn, N. (2016b). 'There's so much data': Exploring the realities of data-based school governance. *European Educational Research Journal*, 15(1), 54–68.

Selwyn, N., Henderson, M. and Chao, S. H. (2015). Exploring the role of digital data in contemporary schools and schooling: '200,000 lines in an Excel spreadsheet'. *British Education Research Journal*, 41(5), 767–781.

Selwyn, N., Hillman, T., Eynon, R., Ferreira, G., Knox, J., Macgilchrist, F., & Sancho-Gil, J. (2020). What's next for Ed-Tech? Critical hopes and concerns for the 2020s. *Learning, Media and Technology*, 45(1), 1–6.

Shain, F. (2010). *The New Folk Devils: Muslim Boys and Education in England*. Stoke-on-Trent: Trentham.

Skelton, C., Francis, B. and Valkanova, Y. (2007). *Breaking Down the Stereotypes: Gender and Achievement in Schools*. Manchester: Equal Opportunities Commission.

Slee, R. (2011). *Irregular Schooling: Special Education, Regular Education and Inclusive Education*. London: Taylor & Francis.

Speck, D. (2020). Ofsted to focus on schools' 'blended learning'. Retrieved 8 July 2020, from https://www.tes.com/news/coronavirus-ofsted-school-visits-focus-blended-learning

Starmer, K. (2020). My Pledges to You. Retrieved 4 July 2020, from https://keirstarmer.com/plans/10-pledges/

Stewart, W. (2021). Revealed: Ofsted's Covid safety plan for school visits. Retrieved 12 January 2021, from https://www.tes.com/news/revealed-ofsteds-covid-safety-plan-school-visits

Stobart, G. (2008). *Testing Times: The Uses and Abuses of Assessment*. London: Routledge.

Strand, S. (2014). Ethnicity, gender, social class and achievement gaps at age 16: Intersectionality and 'getting it' for the white working class. *Research Papers in Education*, 29(2), 131–171.

Strand, S. and Lindorff, A. (2018). Ethnic disproportionality in the identification of Special Educational Needs (SEN) in England: Extent, causes and consequences. University of Oxford. Retrieved 7 January 2021 from https://ora.ox.ac.uk/objects/uuid:a28b7858-994a-4474-9c4b-6962d1f6da41/download_file?file_format=pdf&safe_filename=Strand%2B%2526%2BLindorff_2018_Ethnic%2Bdisproportionality%2B%2526%2BSEN_Report.pdf&type_of_work=Report

Sunderland, M. (n.d.). Child diagnosis: the need to be trauma informed. Retrieved 25 January 2019, from https://senmagazine.co.uk/home/articles/senarticles-2/child-diagnosis-the-need-to-be-trauma-informed

Sveinsson, K. (ed) (2009). *Who Cares About the White Working Class?* London: Runnymede Trust.

Taylor, B., Francis, B., Craig, N., Archer, L., Hodgen, J., Mazenod, A., Tereshchenko, A. and Pepper, D. (2019). Why is it difficult for schools to establish equitable practices in allocating students to attainment 'sets'? *British Journal of Educational Studies*, 67(1), 5–24.

Taylor, E., Gillborn, D. and Ladson-Billings, G. (2009). *Foundations of Critical Race Theory in Education.* London: Routledge.

Taylor-Mullings, N. (2018). *Race, Education and the Status Quo.* Unpublished PhD Thesis, University College London.

Teacher Workload Advisory Group (2018). Making Data Work: Report of the Teacher Workload Advisory Group. Retrieved 21 June 2020, from https://assets.publishing.service.gov.uk/government/uploads/system/uploads/attachment_data/file/754349/Workload_Advisory_Group-report.pdf

TES (2017). Is growth mindset the new learning styles? Retrieved 3 June 2017, from https://www.tes.com/news/weekend-read-growth-mindset-new-learning-styles

The National College (2020). The Recovery Curriculum for Primary Schools: Re-connection, Recovery and Resilience. Retrieved 4 July 2020, from https://thenationalcollege.co.uk/webinars/recovery-curriculum

Thompson, G. and Cook, I. (2014). Manipulating the data: Teaching and NAPLAN in the control society. *Discourse: Studies in the Cultural Politics of Education*, 35(1), 129–142.

Tierney, S. (2020). Is it time to reboot our entire exams system? Retrieved 21 October 2020, from https://www.tes.com/news/it-time-reboot-our-entire-exams-system

Times (2020). Scrap Sats this year – just let kids learn. Retrieved 21 October 2020, from https://www.thetimes.co.uk/article/scrap-sats-this-year-just-let-kids-learn-9qp8kn9rc

Timpson, E. (2019). Foreword to Timpson Review of School Exclusion. Retrieved 9 July 2020, from https://assets.publishing.service.gov.uk/government/uploads/system/uploads/attachment_data/file/807862/Timpson_review.pdf

TIS (n.d.). School Inductions. Retrieved 25 January 2019, from https://www.traumainformedschools.co.uk/school-inductions

Tomlinson, S. (2016). Race, class, ability and school reform. In S. A. Annamma (ed), *DisCrit: Disability Studies and Critical Race Theory in Education*. New York, NY: Teachers College Press.

Tomlinson, S. (2019). *Education and Race from Empire to Brexit*. Bristol: Policy Press.

Towers, E., Taylor, B., Tereshchenko, A. and Mazenod, A. (2020). 'The reality is complex': Teachers' and school leaders' accounts and justifications of grouping practices in the English key stage 2 classroom. *Education 3–13*, 48(1), 22–36.

Trauma Informed Schools (n.d.). Homepage. Retrieved 25 January 2019, from https://www.traumainformedschools.co.uk/

Travers, M.-C. (2017). *White Working-class Boys: Teachers Matter*. London: Trentham Books.

UCL (2020). UCL announces action to acknowledge and address historical links with eugenics. Retrieved 14 June 2020, from https://www.ucl.ac.uk/news/2020/feb/ucl-announces-action-acknowledge-and-address-historical-links-eugenics

UK Government (2019a). Early years foundation stage profile results: 2018 to 2019. Retrieved 4 July 2020, from https://www.gov.uk/government/statistics/early-years-foundation-stage-profile-results-2018-to-2019

UK Government (2019b). Ofsted's new inspection arrangements to focus on curriculum, behaviour and development. Retrieved 13 July 2019, from https://www.gov.uk/government/news/ofsteds-new-inspection-arrangements-to-focus-on-curriculum-behaviour-and-development

UK Government (2019c). Permanent and fixed period exclusions in England 2017 to 2018. Retrieved 9 July 2020, from https://www.gov.uk/government/statistics/permanent-and-fixed-period-exclusions-in-england-2017-to-2018

UK Government (2020a). Ethnicity facts and figures: Development goals for 4 to 5 year olds. Retrieved 4 July 2020, from https://www.ethnicity-facts-figures.service.gov.uk/education-skills-and-training/early-years/attainment-of-development-goals-by-children-aged-4-to-5-years/latest#by-ethnicity-gender-and-eligibility-for-free-school-meals

UK Government (2020b). Ethnicity facts and figures: Reading, writing and maths results for 10 to 11 year olds. Retrieved 5 July 2020 from https://www.ethnicity-facts-figures.service.gov.uk/education-skills-and-training/7-to-11-years-old/reading-writing-and-maths-attainments-for-children-aged-7-to-11-key-stage-2/latest

UK Government (2020c). Key stage 4 performance 2019 (revised). Retrieved 8 July 2020, from https://www.gov.uk/government/statistics/key-stage-4-performance-2019-revised

UK Parliament (2020). Register of All-Party Parliamentary Groups. Retrieved 14 June 2020, from https://publications.parliament.uk/pa/cm/cmallparty/200520/conception-to-age-two---first-1001-days.htm

van Ommen, C. (2013). Book review: *Critical Neuroscience: A Handbook of the Social and Cultural Contexts of Neuroscience. Journal of Theoretical and Philosophical Psychology,* 33(3), 199–202.

VandenBroeck, M. (2017). *Constructions of Neuroscience in Early Childhood Education.* Abingdon: Routledge.

Vandenbroeck, M. and Olsson, L. M. (2017). Discussion. In M. Vandenbroeck (ed), *Constructions of Neuroscience in Early Childhood Education* (pp. 82–92). Abingdon: Routledge.

Vincent, C. and Ball, S. (2007). 'Making up' the middle-class child: Families, activities and class dispositions. *Sociology,* 41(6), 1061–1077.

Walkerdine, V. and Ringrose, J. (2006). Femininities: Reclassifying upward mobility and the neo-liberal subject. In C. Skelton, B. Francis and L. Smulyan (eds), *The Sage Handbook of Gender and Education.* London: Sage.

Ward, H. (2018). 12 organisations shunned baseline bid. Retrieved 5 August 2018, from https://www.tes.com/news/exclusive-12-organisations-shunned-baseline-bid-0

Wastell, D. and White, S. (2012). Blinded by neuroscience: Social policy, the family and the infant brain. *Families, Relationships and Societies,* 1(3), 397–414.

Watt, N. (2013). Boris Johnson invokes Thatcher spirit with greed is good speech. Retrieved 28 June 2020, from https://www.theguardian.com/politics/2013/nov/27/boris-johnson-thatcher-greed-good

Weale, S., Bakare, L. and Mir, S. (2020). Calls grow for black history to be taught to all English school pupils. Retrieved 6 July 2020, from https://www.theguardian.com/education/2020/jun/08/calls-mount-for-black-history-to-be-taught-to-all-uk-school-pupils

White, J. (2006). *Intelligence, Destiny and Education: The Ideological Roots of Intelligence Testing.* London: Routledge.

White, S. and Wastell, D. (2017). Using your brain: Child development, parenting and politics of evidence. In M. Vandenbroeck, J. De Vos, W. Fias, L. M. Olsson and H. Penn (eds), *Constructions of Neuroscience in Early Childhood Education* (pp. 37–53). Abingdon: Routledge.

Whitebread, D. and Bingham, S. (2012). TACTYC Occasional Paper No. 2: School Readiness; a critical review of perspectives and evidence.

Whittaker, F. (2021). SATs scapped in 2021, Williamson confirms. Retrieved 6 January 2021, from https://schoolsweek.co.uk/sats-scapped-in-2021-williamson-confirms/

Wilkins, C. (2011). Professionalism and the post-performative teacher: New teachers reflect on autonomy and accountability in the English school system. *Professional Development in Education*, 37(3), 389–409.

Williamson, B. (2014). Reassembling children as data doppelgangers: How databases are making education machine-readable, *Powerful Knowledge Conference*. University of Bristol.

Williamson, B. (2015). Digital education governance: Data visualization, predictive analytics, and 'real-time' policy instruments. *Journal of Education Policy*, 31(2), 123–141.

Williamson, B. (2017). Decoding ClassDojo: Psycho-policy, social-emotional learning and persuasive educational technologies. *Learning, Media and Technology*, 1–14.

Williamson, B. (2019). Psychodata: Disassembling the psychological, economic, and statistical infrastructure of 'social-emotional learning'. *Journal of Education Policy*, 1–26.

Williamson, B. and Piattoeva, N. (2019). Objectivity as standardization in data-scientific education policy, technology and governance. *Learning, Media and Technology*, 44(1), 64–76.

Williamson, B., Bayne, S. and Shay, S. (2020). The datafication of teaching in Higher Education: Critical issues and perspectives. *Teaching in Higher Education*, 25(4), 351–365.

Williamson, B., Eynon, R. and Potter, J. (2020). Pandemic politics, pedagogies and practices: Digital technologies and distance education during the coronavirus emergency. *Learning, Media and Technology*, 45(2), 107–114.

Williamson, B., Pykett, J. and Nemorin, S. (2018). Biosocial spaces and neurocomputational governance: Brain-based and brain-targeted technologies in education. *Discourse: Studies in the Cultural Politics of Education*, 39(2), 258–275.

Williamson, G. (2020). Education Secretary's statement on coronavirus (COVID-19): 16 May. Retrieved 14 June 2020, from https://www.gov.uk/government/speeches/education-secretarys-statement-on-coronavirus-covid-19-16-may

Wintour, P. (2013). Genetics outweighs teaching, Gove adviser tells his boss. Retrieved 14 June 2020, from https://www.theguardian.com/politics/2013/oct/11/genetics-teaching-gove-adviser

Wintour, P. (2015). Labour must do more to cater for gifted children, says Tristram Hunt. Retrieved 28 June 2020, from https://www.theguardian.com/politics/2015/mar/02/labour-help-gifted-children-tristram-hunt

Wrigley, T. (2019). The zombie theory of genetic intelligence. *FORUM: For Promoting 3–19 Comprehensive Education*, 61, 77–82.

Wyse, D., Bradbury, A., Manyukhina, Y., Sing, S., Ansell, W. and Ozdzynska, M. (2020). Written evidence submitted by Helen Hamlyn Centre for Pedagogy, UCL Institute of Education to the House of Commons Education Select Committee Inquiry: The impact of COVID-19 on education and children's services. Retrieved 15 July 2020, from https://committees.parliament.uk/writtenevidence/6364/pdf/

Yarker, P. (2019). Calling time on 'fixed-ability' thinking and practice. *FORUM: For Promoting 3–19 Comprehensive Education*, 61(1), 3–10.

Yelland, N. (ed). (2010). *Contemporary Perspectives on Early Childhood Education*. Maidenhead: Open University Press.

Youdell, D. (2004). Engineering school markets, constituting schools and subjectivating students: The bureaucratic, institutional and classroom dimensions of educational triage. *Journal of Education Policy*, 19(4), 407–431.

Youdell, D. (2006). *Impossible Bodies, Impossible Selves: Exclusions and Student Subjectivities*. Dordrecht: Springer.

Youdell, D. (2011). *School Trouble: Identity, Power and Politics in Education*. London: Routledge.

Youdell, D. (2016). New biological sciences, sociology and education. *British Journal of Sociology of Education*, 37(5), 788–800.

Youdell, D. (2017). Bioscience and the sociology of education: The case for biosocial education. *British Journal of Sociology of Education*, 38, 1273–1287.

Youdell, D. and Lindley, M. (2018). *Biosocial Education: The Social and Biological Entanglements of Learning*. London: Routledge.

Youdell, D., Harwood, V. and Lindley, M. (2018). Biological sciences, social sciences and the languages of stress. *Discourse: Studies in the Cultural Politics of Education*, 39(2), 219–241.

# Index

References to figures and tables appear in *italic* type. References to endnotes show both the page number and the note number (231n3).

www.ingramcontent.com/pod-product-compliance
Lightning Source LLC
Chambersburg PA
CBHW070932030426
42336CB00014BA/2633